The Enigma of Liechtenstein's Secret Banking System: A Diplomat's Guide

Copyright Page

TITLE: The Enigma of Liechtenstein's Secret Banking System: A Diplomat's Guide

1ST Edition

ISBN: 9798223582014

Table of Contents

The Enigma of Liechtenstein's Secret Banking System: A Diplomat's Guide

By Roberto Miguel Rodriguez

Chapter 1: Liechtenstein: A Secret Banking System in a Fairy Tale Semi-constitutional Monarchy

The Enigmatic Charm of Liechtenstein's Banking System

Liechtenstein, a small yet enchanting country nestled in the heart of Europe, is renowned for its secret banking system, which has captivated the attention of diplomats and economists alike. In this subchapter, we delve into the enigma that is Liechtenstein's banking system, exploring its unique features, benefits, and the role it plays in the country's fairy tale semi-constitutional monarchy.

Liechtenstein's secret banking system is a testament to the nation's commitment to privacy, discretion, and stability. With a long-standing tradition of banking excellence, Liechtenstein has become a renowned hub for offshore banking services, offering a safe haven for individuals and corporations seeking to protect their wealth and assets.

Wealth management and private banking in Liechtenstein are key pillars of its banking system. With a wide range of tailored services, sophisticated investment strategies, and access to global markets, Liechtenstein banks provide unrivaled expertise to affluent clients. The country's favorable tax optimization strategies further enhance its appeal, allowing individuals and businesses to optimize their financial affairs while remaining compliant with international regulations.

Asset protection and trust services are another integral part of Liechtenstein's banking landscape. The country's robust legal framework and trust laws make it an ideal jurisdiction for safeguarding assets and ensuring their seamless transfer across generations. Estate planning and inheritance solutions in Liechtenstein offer a unique blend of security and flexibility, allowing families to preserve their wealth and pass it on to future generations.

Liechtenstein's banking system also presents lucrative investment opportunities. Its financial sector, characterized by stability, innovation, and a strong regulatory framework, attracts savvy investors from around the world. Whether it's venture capital, real estate, or renewable energy projects, Liechtenstein offers a wealth of investment options that promise attractive returns.

What sets Liechtenstein apart is the pivotal role played by its royal family in maintaining the secrecy and stability of its banking system. The royal family's commitment to upholding the country's reputation and ensuring the integrity of its financial sector has garnered deep trust and confidence from clients worldwide.

For diplomats and economists seeking to understand the intricacies of Liechtenstein's banking system, a comprehensive understanding of the regulatory framework and compliance measures is crucial. Liechtenstein's commitment to strict regulations and international cooperation ensures that its banking system remains transparent, compliant, and resilient in the face of global challenges.

Moreover, Liechtenstein's banking system has become a catalyst for wealthy individuals and families considering relocation. The country's exceptional banking services, combined with its high standard of living, political stability, and natural beauty, make it an irresistible destination for those seeking a harmonious blend of financial prosperity and a fairy tale lifestyle.

Lastly, Liechtenstein's banking system facilitates international business transactions, serving as a bridge between various global markets. Its sophisticated infrastructure, along with the country's commitment to innovation and technological advancement, makes Liechtenstein a preferred destination for international trade and investment.

In conclusion, Liechtenstein's secret banking system is an enigmatic charm that continues to captivate diplomats and economists alike. With its fairy tale semi-constitutional monarchy, offshore banking services, wealth management solutions, tax optimization strategies, and a commitment to privacy and stability, Liechtenstein stands as a testament to the enduring allure of its banking system. Whether it's asset protection, investment opportunities, or estate planning, Liechtenstein offers a world-class banking environment that is both secure and prosperous.

The Historical Evolution of Liechtenstein's Banking Sector

Liechtenstein, a tiny principality nestled between Switzerland and Austria, is renowned for its secretive and robust banking system. In this subchapter, we will delve into the historical evolution of Liechtenstein's banking sector and explore how it has become a global leader in offshore banking and wealth management.

Liechtenstein's banking sector traces its roots back to the early 19th century when the principality experienced a period of economic transformation. In 1861, Liechtenstein's first bank, the Liechtensteinische Landesbank, was established as a joint-stock company to meet the growing banking needs of the local population. This marked the beginning of Liechtenstein's journey towards becoming a prominent financial hub.

The geopolitical landscape of the 20th century played a significant role in shaping Liechtenstein's banking sector. During both World Wars, Liechtenstein's neutrality and stable political climate attracted wealthy individuals and families seeking to safeguard their assets. The principality's banking system, built on a foundation of confidentiality and trust, became a haven for those looking to protect their wealth from political and economic uncertainties.

In the 20th century, Liechtenstein's banking sector underwent significant diversification. The introduction of new banking laws in the 1960s and 1970s opened the doors for offshore banking services, attracting international clients seeking tax optimization strategies and asset protection. Liechtenstein's banks began offering comprehensive wealth management and private banking services, catering to the specific needs of affluent individuals and families.

Over the years, Liechtenstein has developed a comprehensive regulatory framework and compliance system to ensure integrity and stability in its banking sector. The Financial Market Authority (FMA) acts as the primary regulatory body, overseeing the activities of banks and ensuring compliance with international standards.

The banking sector's success can also be attributed to Liechtenstein's semi-constitutional monarchy and the role of its royal family. The royal family has played a crucial role in maintaining the secrecy and stability of the banking system, fostering a sense of trust and confidence among clients.

Today, Liechtenstein's banking sector continues to thrive, offering a wide range of services to international clients. Its banks provide investment opportunities in the financial sector, facilitate international business transactions, and offer specialized services such as asset protection, trust services, and estate planning.

In conclusion, Liechtenstein's banking sector has evolved over the years, adapting to changing global dynamics and emerging as a leading player in offshore banking and wealth management. Its rich history, regulatory framework, and commitment to confidentiality have made it an attractive destination for wealthy individuals, families, and international businesses seeking financial services tailored to their unique needs.

The Unique Political Structure of Liechtenstein and its Influence on Banking Secrecy

Liechtenstein, a small European nation nestled between Switzerland and Austria, is often regarded as a fairy tale semi-constitutional monarchy. While its picturesque landscapes and charming castles contribute to this perception, it is the country's unique political structure that has a profound influence on its renowned banking secrecy.

In Liechtenstein, the political power is divided between the reigning Prince and the elected Parliament. This unusual setup allows for a delicate balance between the monarchy's stability and the democratic principles upheld by the Parliament. This structure plays a crucial role in maintaining the secrecy that has made Liechtenstein's banking system so attractive to the global elite.

The monarchy's involvement in the banking system is not merely symbolic. The reigning Prince, as the head of state, has the authority to appoint members to the Financial Market Authority, the regulatory body overseeing the banking sector. This appointment power ensures a close relationship between the monarchy and the financial industry, enabling a certain level of trust and confidentiality.

Furthermore, Liechtenstein's semi-constitutional monarchy contributes to the stability of its banking system. The monarchy provides a sense of continuity and long-term vision, which reassures investors and clients. Stability is a crucial factor for those seeking offshore banking services, wealth management, and private banking in Liechtenstein.

The regulatory framework and compliance in Liechtenstein's banking system are also influenced by its political structure. The Parliament, elected by the people, has the power to legislate and enact laws that govern the financial sector. This democratic oversight ensures that the banking system operates within legal boundaries while still maintaining the necessary secrecy and discretion.

The role of Liechtenstein's royal family cannot be overlooked when discussing the secrecy and stability of its banking system. The royal family has a vested interest in maintaining the integrity of the financial sector, as it contributes significantly to the country's economy. Their commitment to maintaining the secrecy of the banking system is seen as a matter of national importance.

In conclusion, Liechtenstein's unique political structure, characterized by a semi-constitutional monarchy and a democratic Parliament, plays a crucial role in shaping its banking secrecy. The close relationship between the monarchy and the financial industry, the stability provided by the monarchy, and the democratic oversight of the Parliament all contribute to the allure of Liechtenstein's secret banking system. Diplomats and economists seeking offshore banking services, wealth management, and investment opportunities will find Liechtenstein's political structure and its influence on banking secrecy to be a fascinating subject of study.

The Role of Liechtenstein's Royal Family in Maintaining Banking Secrecy

Liechtenstein, a picturesque fairy tale semi-constitutional monarchy nestled in the heart of Europe, is renowned for its secret banking system. Diplomats and economists alike are intrigued by the enigma surrounding this small nation's financial sector, and one cannot fully comprehend the intricacies of Liechtenstein's banking system without understanding the pivotal role played by its royal family in maintaining banking secrecy.

For centuries, Liechtenstein's royal family, the House of Liechtenstein, has been the driving force behind the country's banking system. As the ruling family, they have worked tirelessly to ensure the stability, secrecy, and attractiveness of Liechtenstein as an offshore financial center. The House of Liechtenstein's unwavering commitment to the preservation of banking secrecy has made the country a favored destination for wealthy individuals, families, and businesses seeking to safeguard their assets.

The royal family has played a crucial role in shaping the regulatory framework and compliance measures of Liechtenstein's banking system. Their extensive knowledge and experience have guided the development of laws and regulations that strike a delicate balance between protecting the privacy of clients and preventing illicit activities such as money laundering and tax evasion. The House of Liechtenstein's active involvement in the legislative process ensures that the country's banking system remains transparent, trustworthy, and compliant with international standards.

Moreover, the royal family's reputation and global network have contributed to the growth of Liechtenstein's financial sector. Their personal connections with influential individuals, diplomats, and entrepreneurs have facilitated lucrative investment opportunities and international business transactions. The House of Liechtenstein's endorsement of the country's banking system has attracted wealthy individuals and families seeking to relocate to Liechtenstein for its exceptional wealth management and private banking services.

In addition to their role in the banking sector, the royal family has been instrumental in promoting the estate planning and inheritance solutions offered by Liechtenstein. Their expertise in trust services and asset protection has made Liechtenstein an attractive destination for individuals looking to preserve their wealth for future generations.

The House of Liechtenstein's dedication to maintaining the secrecy and stability of Liechtenstein's banking system cannot be overstated. Their involvement in the country's financial sector goes beyond mere figureheads; they are active participants in shaping policies, establishing international relationships, and ensuring the long-term viability of Liechtenstein as a premier offshore banking destination.

In conclusion, the role of Liechtenstein's royal family in maintaining banking secrecy is indispensable. Their commitment to secrecy, stability, and compliance has solidified Liechtenstein's reputation as a trusted and sought-after destination for offshore banking services, wealth management, and asset protection. Diplomats and economists must appreciate the invaluable contribution of the royal family in understanding the unique nature of Liechtenstein's secret banking system.

Chapter 2: Offshore Banking Services in Liechtenstein

Understanding Offshore Banking and its Advantages

Offshore banking has long been a topic of interest for diplomats and economists, particularly within the context of Liechtenstein's secret banking system. In this subchapter, we will delve into the intricacies of offshore banking and explore its advantages, specifically within the unique framework of Liechtenstein's fairy tale semi-constitutional monarchy.

Liechtenstein: A Secret Banking System in a Fairy Tale Semi-constitutional Monarchy

Liechtenstein's banking system has often been dubbed as a fairy tale due to its seemingly magical ability to maintain utmost secrecy and stability. This section will shed light on the historical context and the unique factors that contribute to the allure of Liechtenstein's banking system.

Offshore Banking Services in Liechtenstein

Liechtenstein offers a range of offshore banking services, catering to the needs of high-net-worth individuals and international businesses. From private banking to wealth management, this section will explore the comprehensive offerings available in Liechtenstein's offshore banking sector.

Wealth Management and Private Banking in Liechtenstein

Liechtenstein's offshore banking services are renowned for their expertise in wealth management and private banking. This subchapter will delve into the advantages of entrusting one's assets to Liechtenstein's skilled professionals and the bespoke solutions they offer.

Tax Optimization Strategies in Liechtenstein

One of the key advantages of offshore banking in Liechtenstein is the opportunity for tax optimization. Diplomats and economists will find valuable insights into the legal strategies available to maximize tax efficiency while complying with international regulations.

Asset Protection and Trust Services in Liechtenstein

Liechtenstein's offshore banking system provides robust asset protection and trust services. This section will explore the intricacies of establishing trusts and the benefits they offer in terms of asset safeguarding and inheritance planning.

Investment Opportunities in Liechtenstein's Financial Sector

Liechtenstein's financial sector presents a wealth of investment opportunities. Diplomats and economists will gain an understanding of the diverse investment options available within the secure and stable environment of Liechtenstein.

Regulatory Framework and Compliance in Liechtenstein's Banking System

Liechtenstein's banking system operates within a well-regulated framework, ensuring compliance with international standards. This subchapter will elucidate the regulatory policies and mechanisms that contribute to the system's integrity.

Wealthy Individuals and Families Relocating to Liechtenstein for its Banking System

Liechtenstein's appeal extends beyond offshore banking services. This section will highlight the advantages that attract wealthy individuals and families to relocate to Liechtenstein, including the country's banking system and its associated benefits.

Estate Planning and Inheritance Solutions in Liechtenstein

Liechtenstein's offshore banking system offers comprehensive estate planning and inheritance solutions. Diplomats and economists will gain insights into the advantages of utilizing Liechtenstein's expertise in this domain.

International Business Transactions Facilitated through Liechtenstein's Banking System

Liechtenstein's banking system plays a pivotal role in enabling international business transactions. This subchapter will explore the mechanisms that make Liechtenstein an attractive hub for cross-border business endeavors.

The Role of Liechtenstein's Royal Family in Maintaining the Secrecy and Stability of its Banking System

The secrecy and stability of Liechtenstein's banking system are intricately tied to the role played by the royal family. This section will shed light on the historical context and the ongoing contributions of the royal family in maintaining the system's integrity.

In conclusion, this subchapter provides diplomats and economists with a comprehensive understanding of offshore banking and its advantages within Liechtenstein's secret banking system. From wealth management to tax optimization and international business transactions, Liechtenstein offers a range of services tailored to the needs of its esteemed clientele. Whether one is an investor, a family looking for asset protection, or a business seeking international opportunities, Liechtenstein's banking system is a gateway to financial prosperity within a fairy tale semi-constitutional monarchy.

The Appeal of Liechtenstein as an Offshore Banking Destination

Liechtenstein, a small fairy tale semi-constitutional monarchy nestled between Switzerland and Austria, has long been recognized as a haven for the world's wealthy elite seeking the utmost discretion and stability in their financial affairs. With its secret banking system, Liechtenstein has become a magnet for diplomats and economists seeking to understand and tap into the unique offerings of this tiny principality.

One of the primary reasons why Liechtenstein holds such appeal as an offshore banking destination is its unrivaled commitment to privacy and confidentiality. The country's banking system is shrouded in secrecy, providing a safe haven for individuals and corporations alike who wish to protect their assets from prying eyes and potential legal disputes. Liechtenstein's strong legal framework and strict adherence to international banking regulations ensure that its clients' financial affairs remain strictly confidential.

Furthermore, Liechtenstein's offshore banking services are renowned for their exceptional wealth management and private banking offerings. The country boasts a highly skilled and experienced workforce, comprised of financial experts who specialize in tailoring customized solutions to meet the unique needs of each client. Whether it is investment advice, asset diversification, or tax optimization strategies, Liechtenstein's banking system provides a comprehensive suite of services to help clients safeguard and grow their wealth.

In addition to wealth management, Liechtenstein also offers a range of asset protection and trust services. These services are particularly attractive to high-net-worth individuals and families looking to shield their assets from potential risks, such as lawsuits or bankruptcy. Liechtenstein's trust laws are among the most robust and flexible in the world, offering clients a wide array of options for safeguarding their wealth for future generations.

Moreover, Liechtenstein's financial sector presents lucrative investment opportunities for those looking to capitalize on the country's stable economy and favorable business environment. The principality's well-regulated banking system, coupled with its low tax rates and attractive investment incentives, make it an ideal destination for individuals and corporations seeking to grow their wealth through strategic investments.

It is worth noting that Liechtenstein's banking system operates within a stringent regulatory framework, ensuring compliance with international standards. The country's commitment to transparency and adherence to global regulations has earned it a reputation as a responsible and reliable financial center.

The role of Liechtenstein's royal family cannot be overlooked when considering the appeal of the country's banking system. The royal family has played a significant role in maintaining the secrecy and stability of Liechtenstein's banking sector. Their unwavering support and commitment to the principality's financial institutions have instilled trust and confidence in clients worldwide.

In conclusion, Liechtenstein's secret banking system offers a unique blend of privacy, stability, and wealth management services that make it an attractive offshore banking destination for diplomats and economists alike. Whether it is tax optimization strategies, asset protection, or investment opportunities, Liechtenstein's banking system provides an enticing array of services for those seeking to protect and grow their wealth. With its strong regulatory framework and the support of the royal family, Liechtenstein continues to uphold its reputation as a premier destination for individuals and corporations looking for financial peace of mind.

An Overview of Offshore Banking Services Offered in Liechtenstein

Liechtenstein, a small principality nestled in the heart of Europe, has long been regarded as a hub for offshore banking services. Its secretive and stable banking system has attracted wealthy individuals, families, and businesses from around the world seeking to safeguard their assets, optimize their tax strategies, and benefit from the country's robust wealth management and private banking services.

Offshore banking services in Liechtenstein are tailored to meet the diverse needs of its sophisticated clientele. The country offers a wide range of banking solutions, including wealth management and private banking services that cater to individuals and families seeking personalized financial advice and investment strategies. With a strong emphasis on discretion and confidentiality, Liechtenstein's banks provide a safe haven for asset protection and trust services, ensuring that clients' wealth is shielded from prying eyes and potential risks.

Liechtenstein's banking system also offers attractive investment opportunities, with its financial sector providing access to a diverse range of asset classes, including equities, bonds, real estate, and alternative investments. The country's regulatory framework and compliance standards ensure that international business transactions are facilitated smoothly, offering a transparent and secure environment for conducting cross-border transactions.

Moreover, Liechtenstein's banking system has become a favored destination for wealthy individuals and families seeking to relocate and establish residency due to the country's favorable tax optimization strategies. With its low tax rates and wealth-friendly regulations, Liechtenstein offers a unique opportunity for individuals to preserve their wealth and plan for the future through effective estate planning and inheritance solutions.

The role of Liechtenstein's royal family cannot be overlooked when discussing the secrecy and stability of its banking system. The royal family has been instrumental in maintaining the principality's reputation as a safe haven for offshore banking, ensuring that the country's financial institutions adhere to the highest standards of professionalism, integrity, and confidentiality.

In conclusion, Liechtenstein's offshore banking services have firmly established the country as a premier destination for individuals, families, and businesses seeking to protect and grow their wealth. With its comprehensive range of services, favorable tax environment, and strict regulatory framework, Liechtenstein offers a fairy tale-like semi-constitutional monarchy that enables its clients to navigate the complex world of international finance with confidence and peace of mind.

Compliance and Legal Considerations for Offshore Banking in Liechtenstein

Liechtenstein's secret banking system has long been a topic of intrigue and fascination, particularly for diplomats and economists seeking to understand the inner workings of this fairy tale semi-constitutional monarchy. As the global financial landscape evolves, it is crucial for those interested in Liechtenstein's offshore banking services to be aware of the compliance and legal considerations that come with it.

Liechtenstein's banking system is known for its commitment to strict regulatory frameworks and compliance measures. This commitment is not only driven by international standards but also by the need to maintain the secrecy and stability of its banking system. The country has implemented robust anti-money laundering (AML) and know your customer (KYC) procedures to ensure that only legitimate funds flow through its financial institutions.

For diplomats and economists considering Liechtenstein's offshore banking services, it is essential to understand the regulatory framework that governs this sector. Liechtenstein's Financial Market Authority (FMA) is the regulatory authority responsible for overseeing the country's financial sector. This includes ensuring compliance with international standards, such as those set by the Financial Action Task Force (FATF) and the Organization for Economic Cooperation and Development (OECD).

When it comes to wealth management and private banking in Liechtenstein, compliance with tax regulations is a paramount concern. Liechtenstein offers attractive tax optimization strategies for individuals and families, but it is crucial to navigate these strategies within the bounds of legal frameworks. Understanding the tax implications and ensuring compliance is essential to avoid any legal repercussions.

Asset protection and trust services in Liechtenstein are another key aspect of its offshore banking system. Liechtenstein's legal framework provides robust protection for assets held within its jurisdiction, making it an attractive destination for individuals seeking to protect their wealth. However, it is vital to ensure that the asset protection strategies employed are in compliance with international laws to maintain the integrity of these arrangements.

Furthermore, diplomats and economists interested in Liechtenstein's banking system should be aware of the opportunities it offers for investment. Liechtenstein has a diverse financial sector that provides various investment opportunities, including private equity, real estate, and alternative investments. Understanding the regulatory framework surrounding these investments is crucial to ensure compliance and mitigate any potential risks.

Finally, it is worth noting the role of Liechtenstein's royal family in maintaining the secrecy and stability of its banking system. The royal family has played a significant role in promoting the country's financial sector while also upholding its reputation for discretion. Their commitment to maintaining the privacy and security of the banking system is a central pillar of Liechtenstein's offshore banking services.

In conclusion, diplomats and economists interested in Liechtenstein's secret banking system must be well-versed in the compliance and legal considerations that come with offshore banking. Understanding the regulatory framework, tax implications, asset protection strategies, and investment opportunities is crucial to make informed decisions and navigate the complexities of Liechtenstein's banking system successfully. By doing so, they can leverage the benefits and opportunities offered by Liechtenstein's offshore banking services while maintaining compliance with international standards.

Chapter 3: Wealth Management and Private Banking in Liechtenstein

The Importance of Wealth Management in Liechtenstein

Liechtenstein, a small but prosperous monarchy nestled in the heart of Europe, has long been known for its secretive and robust banking system. With its fairy tale-like landscape and semi-constitutional monarchy, the country has attracted the attention of diplomats and economists alike. In this subchapter, we delve into the crucial role that wealth management plays in Liechtenstein's banking system, addressing the specific interests of our target audience.

Liechtenstein offers a range of offshore banking services that cater to the needs of high-net-worth individuals and families. Wealth management and private banking in the country are characterized by a commitment to privacy, confidentiality, and personalized service. By leveraging its strong regulatory framework and compliance measures, Liechtenstein ensures that clients' assets are protected and their wealth is optimized through tax optimization strategies.

One of the key advantages of wealth management in Liechtenstein is the access it provides to asset protection and trust services. The country's robust legal system and well-established trust laws allow individuals and families to safeguard their wealth for future generations. Liechtenstein's banking system also offers a wide range of investment opportunities, enabling clients to diversify their portfolios and achieve long-term financial growth.

Moreover, Liechtenstein's banking system plays a crucial role in facilitating international business transactions. Its well-established infrastructure, combined with the country's reputation for stability and reliability, makes it an ideal hub for cross-border trade and investments.

The banking system also offers estate planning and inheritance solutions that help clients navigate complex legal and tax frameworks, ensuring the smooth transfer of wealth.

In understanding the importance of wealth management in Liechtenstein, one cannot overlook the role of the royal family in maintaining the secrecy and stability of the banking system. The royal family's commitment to upholding the country's reputation and their close ties with the financial sector have been pivotal in attracting wealthy individuals and families seeking a secure and discreet banking environment.

In conclusion, wealth management is of utmost importance in Liechtenstein's banking system. With its emphasis on privacy, asset protection, and personalized service, Liechtenstein has established itself as a leading destination for wealthy individuals and families seeking optimal financial solutions. The country's regulatory framework, investment opportunities, and commitment to maintaining secrecy make it an attractive choice for diplomats and economists looking to understand the enigma of Liechtenstein's secret banking system.

Private Banking Services and Benefits in Liechtenstein

Liechtenstein, a small fairy tale semi-constitutional monarchy nestled in the heart of Europe, is renowned for its secret banking system that has captivated the attention of diplomats and economists alike. This subchapter explores the private banking services and benefits offered by Liechtenstein, drawing attention to the unique opportunities that make it an attractive destination for wealthy individuals, families, and international business transactions.

Liechtenstein's secret banking system is built upon a foundation of offshore banking services that provide a haven for individuals seeking to protect their assets and optimize their tax strategies. The country's wealth management and private banking sector offers a range of services tailored to the needs and preferences of discerning clients. From personalized investment advice to portfolio diversification, Liechtenstein's private banks pride themselves on delivering exceptional financial solutions.

One of the key advantages of banking in Liechtenstein is the robust regulatory framework and compliance measures that ensure the integrity and stability of the system. Diplomats and economists can trust that their funds are secure and protected by stringent standards, enhancing the confidence and peace of mind of those who choose Liechtenstein as their banking destination.

Liechtenstein's banking system also offers a wide range of asset protection and trust services, allowing individuals to safeguard their wealth for future generations. Estate planning and inheritance solutions are readily available, providing comprehensive strategies to manage and transfer wealth effectively.

Moreover, Liechtenstein's financial sector presents enticing investment opportunities for those seeking to diversify their portfolios. With a strong focus on innovation and sustainability, the country's banking system has attracted numerous investors looking to capitalize on emerging markets and industries.

The role of Liechtenstein's royal family cannot be overlooked when discussing the secrecy and stability of its banking system. Their commitment to maintaining the confidentiality and trustworthiness of the country's financial institutions has been instrumental in preserving Liechtenstein's reputation as a premier destination for private banking.

In conclusion, Liechtenstein's secret banking system offers a plethora of services and benefits to diplomats and economists. From offshore banking and wealth management to tax optimization strategies and asset protection, Liechtenstein is an attractive destination for those seeking a secure and confidential banking environment. With its robust regulatory framework, investment opportunities, and inheritance solutions, Liechtenstein continues to be a preferred choice for wealthy individuals, families, and international business transactions.

Investment Strategies and Opportunities in Liechtenstein's Wealth Management Sector

Liechtenstein, a small principality nestled within the heart of Europe, has gained a reputation as a secret banking system that offers a fairy tale-like experience for those seeking offshore banking services. With its semi-constitutional monarchy and a well-regulated financial sector, Liechtenstein has become a haven for wealthy individuals, families, and businesses looking for wealth management and private banking services.

In this subchapter, we will explore the various investment strategies and opportunities available in Liechtenstein's wealth management sector, addressing the interests of diplomats and economists. Liechtenstein offers a range of tailored solutions for tax optimization, asset protection, and trust services, making it an attractive destination for international investors.

One of the key advantages of investing in Liechtenstein's financial sector is the wide array of investment opportunities available. The principality boasts a robust and diverse financial market, providing investors with access to both traditional and alternative asset classes. From equities and bonds to real estate and private equity, Liechtenstein offers a wealth of options to suit different risk appetites and investment goals.

Moreover, Liechtenstein's regulatory framework and compliance standards are known for their stringent nature. The country has established a reputation for maintaining a high level of transparency and adhering to international standards, ensuring the stability and security of its banking system. This level of regulatory oversight provides investors with confidence and peace of mind when considering investment opportunities in Liechtenstein.

Additionally, Liechtenstein's royal family plays a crucial role in maintaining the secrecy and stability of its banking system. Their commitment to upholding privacy laws and maintaining the trust of their clients has been instrumental in attracting wealthy individuals and families to relocate to Liechtenstein. This unique combination of a stable political environment and a well-regulated banking system makes Liechtenstein an ideal destination for those seeking to protect and grow their wealth.

Furthermore, Liechtenstein's wealth management sector offers comprehensive estate planning and inheritance solutions. With a range of services such as family offices and trust structures, individuals can ensure a smooth transition of their wealth to future generations while minimizing tax implications.

Lastly, Liechtenstein's banking system facilitates international business transactions, providing a secure and efficient platform for cross-border trade and investment. The principality's well-established network of correspondent banks and financial institutions enables seamless global financial operations.

In conclusion, Liechtenstein's wealth management sector offers a multitude of investment strategies and opportunities for diplomats and economists alike. With its robust regulatory framework, diverse investment options, and commitment to privacy, Liechtenstein continues to be a sought-after destination for individuals and businesses looking to optimize their wealth and protect their assets.

Strengthening Wealth through Liechtenstein's Private Banking Services

Liechtenstein's private banking services have long been regarded as a cornerstone of the country's secretive and stable banking system. For diplomats and economists seeking to understand the enigma of Liechtenstein's secret banking system, exploring the role of private banking in strengthening wealth is essential.

Liechtenstein, a fairy tale semi-constitutional monarchy, has become synonymous with offshore banking services, attracting high-net-worth individuals and families from around the world. Private banking in Liechtenstein offers a range of bespoke wealth management solutions tailored to the unique needs of each client.

One of the key advantages of Liechtenstein's private banking services is its tax optimization strategies. The country has a favorable tax regime, allowing individuals and businesses to optimize their tax liabilities legally. By leveraging Liechtenstein's tax laws, clients can effectively manage their wealth and minimize their tax burdens.

In addition to tax optimization, Liechtenstein's private banking services also provide asset protection and trust services. Wealthy individuals and families can establish trusts and foundations in Liechtenstein, ensuring the preservation and growth of their assets for future generations. These structures offer enhanced privacy and security, shielding assets from potential risks and uncertainties.

Liechtenstein's private banking sector also offers a wide range of investment opportunities. The country's financial sector is known for its stability and transparency, making it an attractive destination for investors seeking long-term growth and diversification. With a robust regulatory framework and compliance standards, clients can have confidence in the integrity of Liechtenstein's financial system.

Furthermore, Liechtenstein's private banking services play a crucial role in facilitating international business transactions. The country's banks have extensive experience in cross-border transactions, offering efficient and secure solutions for businesses operating globally. With their expertise in international finance, Liechtenstein's private banks serve as trusted partners for businesses seeking to expand their operations abroad.

It is worth noting that Liechtenstein's royal family has played a significant role in maintaining the secrecy and stability of the country's banking system. The royal family's commitment to upholding the highest standards of discretion and reliability has earned Liechtenstein a reputation as a trustworthy and secure financial hub.

In conclusion, Liechtenstein's private banking services are essential for diplomats and economists seeking to understand the secrets behind the country's banking system. From wealth management and tax optimization to asset protection and international business transactions, Liechtenstein's private banks offer a comprehensive suite of services that strengthen wealth and secure financial futures. By leveraging the expertise and advantages of Liechtenstein's private banking sector, individuals and businesses can navigate the complexities of global finance with confidence.

Chapter 4: Tax Optimization Strategies in Liechtenstein

Liechtenstein's Tax System and its Benefits for Foreign Investors

Liechtenstein, a fairy tale semi-constitutional monarchy nestled in the heart of Europe, boasts a secret banking system that has captivated the attention of diplomats and economists alike. In this subchapter, we delve into Liechtenstein's tax system and explore the numerous benefits it offers to foreign investors.

When it comes to offshore banking services, Liechtenstein has established itself as a premier destination. One of the key attractions for foreign investors is the country's favorable tax regime. Liechtenstein operates a territorial tax system, which means that taxes are only levied on income generated within its borders. This allows foreign investors to enjoy a highly advantageous tax environment, as income earned outside of Liechtenstein remains untaxed.

Wealth management and private banking in Liechtenstein have also flourished thanks to its tax optimization strategies. The country offers a wide range of tax planning options, such as the establishment of foundations and trusts, which provide significant asset protection benefits. These structures allow investors to safeguard their wealth and enjoy favorable tax treatment, ensuring the preservation and growth of their assets.

Furthermore, Liechtenstein's regulatory framework and compliance in its banking system are renowned for their robustness. The country has implemented stringent regulations to combat money laundering and ensure transparency. This commitment to regulatory compliance has not only strengthened the integrity of Liechtenstein's banking system but also fostered trust and confidence among investors.

Foreign investors looking to relocate to Liechtenstein for its banking system can also benefit from its estate planning and inheritance solutions. Liechtenstein offers a range of specialized services, including the establishment of family trusts and foundations, facilitating the seamless transfer of wealth across generations. These solutions provide a secure and efficient way to manage family assets and plan for future generations.

Liechtenstein's financial sector also presents attractive investment opportunities. The country has a well-developed and diversified economy, with a strong focus on sectors such as finance, technology, and manufacturing. Foreign investors can tap into these sectors and benefit from Liechtenstein's stable political climate, highly skilled workforce, and well-established infrastructure.

The role of Liechtenstein's royal family cannot be overlooked when discussing the secrecy and stability of its banking system. The principality's royal family has been instrumental in maintaining the confidentiality and trust that underpins Liechtenstein's financial sector. Their longstanding commitment to preserving the country's reputation and upholding the highest standards of governance has been crucial in attracting foreign investors.

In conclusion, Liechtenstein's tax system offers an array of benefits for foreign investors. From its favorable tax regime and tax optimization strategies to its robust regulatory framework and compliance, Liechtenstein provides a secure and advantageous environment for wealth management, investment, and international business transactions. Combined with its estate planning solutions and the role of its royal family, Liechtenstein's secret banking system continues to be a magnet for diplomats and economists seeking financial opportunities in a fairy tale setting.

Tax Planning and Optimization Techniques in Liechtenstein

Liechtenstein, often regarded as a fairy tale semi-constitutional monarchy, is widely recognized for its secret banking system. This enigmatic nation has become a preferred destination for wealthy individuals, families, and businesses seeking offshore banking services, wealth management, and private banking solutions. One of the key advantages Liechtenstein offers is its robust tax optimization strategies.

For diplomats and economists delving into Liechtenstein's secret banking system, understanding the tax planning and optimization techniques is crucial. Liechtenstein provides a range of legal strategies to minimize tax liabilities, making it an attractive jurisdiction for international investors.

One of the most prominent tax optimization strategies offered in Liechtenstein is the use of asset protection and trust services. These services allow individuals to safeguard their assets from potential risks while reducing tax burdens. By setting up trusts, individuals can separate their assets from personal ownership, thus enjoying favorable tax treatment.

Liechtenstein's banking system also offers various investment opportunities. The financial sector provides a wide range of investment products and services, including private equity, real estate, and hedge funds. These investment opportunities not only allow for diversification but also offer tax advantages such as lower withholding taxes and capital gains tax exemptions.

In addition to investment opportunities, Liechtenstein's regulatory framework and compliance standards ensure transparency and adherence to international tax regulations. Diplomats and economists can be assured that Liechtenstein's banking system operates within a strict legal framework, reducing the risk of tax evasion and illicit activities.

Furthermore, Liechtenstein's banking system attracts wealthy individuals and families who are considering relocating for its banking services. The stability and secrecy offered by Liechtenstein's royal family play a crucial role in maintaining the trust of these individuals. Their commitment to preserving the nation's banking system's integrity ensures the confidentiality and security of clients' financial assets.

Estate planning and inheritance solutions are also key considerations for individuals utilizing Liechtenstein's banking system. The country's legal framework allows for efficient and tax-optimized transfer of wealth across generations, providing peace of mind to individuals concerned about their heirs' financial security and tax implications.

Lastly, Liechtenstein's banking system facilitates international business transactions, offering a gateway for businesses to expand their global reach. The nation's financial infrastructure, combined with its tax optimization strategies, makes it an ideal hub for international trade and investment.

In conclusion, Liechtenstein's secret banking system offers a myriad of tax planning and optimization techniques. Diplomats and economists exploring this topic will discover a range of strategies, including asset protection and trust services, investment opportunities, estate planning solutions, and compliance with international tax regulations. Liechtenstein's royal family plays a crucial role in maintaining the secrecy and stability of the banking system, making it an attractive destination for wealthy individuals, families, and businesses seeking financial services with a focus on tax optimization.

Case Studies on Successful Tax Optimization in Liechtenstein

Liechtenstein, a tiny landlocked country nestled between Switzerland and Austria, has long been renowned for its secretive and robust banking system. With its fairy tale-like semi-constitutional monarchy and favorable tax environment, Liechtenstein has attracted a diverse range of individuals and businesses seeking to optimize their tax liabilities. In this subchapter, we will explore some compelling case studies that illustrate successful tax optimization strategies employed in Liechtenstein.

Case Study 1: Mr. Smith, an American entrepreneur, sought to minimize his tax burden while maintaining the confidentiality of his financial affairs. By establishing a trust in Liechtenstein, Mr. Smith was able to transfer his assets to the trust, thereby legally separating them from his personal ownership. As a result, he significantly reduced his taxable income, as the trust was subject to more favorable tax treatment. Furthermore, the anonymity provided by Liechtenstein's banking system ensured Mr. Smith's financial privacy.

Case Study 2: The Johnson family, a wealthy European family, aimed to protect their assets from potential creditors and ensure smooth succession planning. By setting up a family foundation in Liechtenstein, the Johnsons could safeguard their wealth and transfer it to future generations without incurring hefty inheritance taxes. Additionally, the Johnsons utilized the expertise of Liechtenstein's wealth management professionals to diversify their investments and maximize returns.

Case Study 3: Company XYZ, a multinational corporation, sought to streamline its tax structure and benefit from double taxation treaties. By establishing a holding company in Liechtenstein, Company XYZ was able to centralize its global operations and take advantage of the country's extensive network of tax treaties. This enabled the company to reduce its overall tax liability while complying with international tax laws and regulations.

These case studies exemplify the versatility and effectiveness of tax optimization strategies available in Liechtenstein. While each case is unique, they all share a common goal: to leverage Liechtenstein's favorable tax environment, wealth management services, and asset protection mechanisms to achieve financial objectives while maintaining confidentiality.

It is important to note that Liechtenstein's banking system operates within a robust regulatory framework, ensuring compliance with international standards. The country's royal family plays a crucial role in maintaining the secrecy and stability of the banking system, further enhancing Liechtenstein's reputation as a trusted and secure financial hub.

For diplomats and economists seeking to understand Liechtenstein's secret banking system, these case studies provide valuable insights into the various tax optimization strategies employed by individuals and businesses. Whether it is through trusts, foundations, or corporate structures, Liechtenstein offers a range of solutions to meet the diverse needs of its clientele. As the demand for offshore banking services, wealth management, and tax optimization continues to grow, Liechtenstein's financial sector presents attractive investment opportunities for those willing to explore its potential.

Compliance and Ethical Considerations in Tax Optimization Strategies

In the intricate world of Liechtenstein's secret banking system, compliance and ethical considerations play a crucial role in tax optimization strategies. As diplomats and economists delve into the realm of offshore banking services, wealth management, and private banking, it becomes imperative to understand the regulatory framework and the ethical implications involved.

Liechtenstein, with its fairy tale semi-constitutional monarchy, has long been known for its discreet and reliable offshore banking services. However, it is essential to note that while tax optimization strategies are legal, they must be carried out within the boundaries of ethical considerations and compliance with international regulations.

The banking sector in Liechtenstein offers a multitude of tax optimization strategies tailored to the unique needs of wealthy individuals and families. These strategies encompass asset protection, trust services, estate planning, and inheritance solutions. However, it is crucial to ensure that these strategies align with internationally accepted ethical standards.

Liechtenstein's regulatory framework is designed to maintain the secrecy and stability of its banking system, but it also imposes stringent compliance requirements. Diplomats and economists must familiarize themselves with these regulations to ensure that any tax optimization strategies adopted are in full compliance with the law.

Furthermore, ethical considerations should not be overlooked. Wealthy individuals and families relocating to Liechtenstein for its banking system must evaluate the ethical implications of their tax optimization strategies. It is crucial to strike a balance between lawful tax planning and ethical behavior to uphold the integrity of the system.

International business transactions facilitated through Liechtenstein's banking system also require careful consideration of compliance and ethics. Diplomats and economists must navigate the intricacies of cross-border transactions while ensuring adherence to international regulations and ethical standards.

While Liechtenstein's royal family plays a significant role in maintaining the secrecy and stability of its banking system, it is essential to remember that compliance and ethical considerations extend beyond the influence of any single entity. The collective responsibility lies with diplomats, economists, and the banking sector to uphold the highest ethical standards while engaging in tax optimization strategies.

In conclusion, compliance and ethical considerations are integral components of tax optimization strategies within Liechtenstein's secret banking system. Diplomats and economists must navigate the regulatory framework, uphold ethical standards, and ensure full compliance with international regulations. By doing so, they can leverage Liechtenstein's banking system to its fullest potential while maintaining integrity and trust within the global financial community.

Chapter 5: Asset Protection and Trust Services in Liechtenstein

Understanding Asset Protection and its Importance in Liechtenstein

Liechtenstein, a secretive fairy tale semi-constitutional monarchy, is renowned for its robust offshore banking services, wealth management, and private banking. One crucial aspect that sets Liechtenstein apart from other financial hubs is its strong focus on asset protection. This subchapter delves into the concept of asset protection, its significance in Liechtenstein, and how it benefits diplomats, economists, and individuals seeking to safeguard their wealth.

Asset protection refers to the legal strategies and structures used to shield assets from potential risks, such as lawsuits, creditors, or economic uncertainties. In Liechtenstein, the emphasis on asset protection is deeply ingrained in the country's financial system, making it an attractive destination for those desiring to protect their wealth.

Liechtenstein offers a range of trust services that provide individuals with the means to safeguard their assets. Trusts act as legal entities that hold and manage assets on behalf of beneficiaries. They offer a high level of confidentiality, asset segregation, and protection against potential claims. Liechtenstein's trust laws are well-established and provide a solid framework for asset protection.

For diplomats and economists, asset protection in Liechtenstein not only ensures the safety of their wealth but also provides a stable environment for their financial activities. The country's regulatory framework and compliance standards ensure transparency and mitigate risks, which is crucial for individuals involved in international business transactions.

Moreover, Liechtenstein's banking system offers investment opportunities that can further enhance asset protection. The financial sector provides a wide array of investment instruments, including funds, bonds, and real estate, allowing individuals to diversify their portfolios and protect their wealth against market fluctuations.

Furthermore, Liechtenstein's royal family plays a significant role in maintaining the secrecy and stability of its banking system. Their commitment to upholding the country's financial reputation adds an extra layer of trust and security, making Liechtenstein an attractive destination for wealthy individuals and families seeking to relocate.

Estate planning and inheritance solutions are also integral aspects of asset protection in Liechtenstein. The country's laws and regulations enable individuals to structure their assets to ensure a smooth transfer of wealth to future generations, minimizing tax liabilities and protecting their legacies.

In conclusion, understanding asset protection and its importance in Liechtenstein is vital for diplomats and economists seeking to navigate the country's secret banking system. Liechtenstein's focus on asset protection, trust services, investment opportunities, and robust regulatory framework makes it an ideal destination for those looking to safeguard their wealth and engage in international financial activities. By grasping the intricacies of asset protection in Liechtenstein, individuals can make informed decisions and secure their financial future in this unique and secretive financial haven.

Trust Services and Structures Offered in Liechtenstein

Liechtenstein has long been renowned as a hub for offshore banking services, offering a secret banking system that has captivated the interest of diplomats and economists alike. This fairy tale semi-constitutional monarchy has established itself as a prominent player in the global financial landscape, attracting wealthy individuals, families, and businesses seeking specialized wealth management and private banking services.

At the heart of Liechtenstein's banking system lies its extensive range of trust services and structures. These services are designed to offer individuals and corporations alike the opportunity to optimize their tax strategies, protect their assets, and facilitate international business transactions.

One of the key advantages of Liechtenstein's trust services is its robust regulatory framework and compliance standards. The country's financial institutions are subject to stringent regulations, ensuring transparency and accountability in all financial transactions. This regulatory strength has contributed to the stability and reliability of Liechtenstein's banking system, making it an attractive destination for those seeking a secure and discreet location to manage their wealth.

Liechtenstein's trust services go beyond simple asset protection. The country provides comprehensive estate planning and inheritance solutions, allowing individuals and families to effectively manage their succession plans and ensure the smooth transfer of wealth to future generations. With its favorable tax environment, Liechtenstein offers attractive opportunities for tax optimization strategies, enabling individuals and businesses to maximize their financial growth potential.

Furthermore, Liechtenstein's banking system offers investment opportunities that are tailored to the specific needs of its clients. Whether it be private equity, real estate, or alternative investments, Liechtenstein's financial sector provides a wide range of options designed to meet the unique requirements of high-net-worth individuals and businesses.

It is worth noting the crucial role played by Liechtenstein's royal family in maintaining the secrecy and stability of its banking system. The royal family has fostered an environment of trust, ensuring the confidentiality and discretion that is essential to the success of Liechtenstein's banking industry.

In conclusion, Liechtenstein's trust services and structures have positioned the country as a premier destination for individuals and businesses seeking a secure and discreet environment to manage their wealth. With its comprehensive range of services, favorable tax environment, and robust regulatory framework, Liechtenstein offers diplomats and economists a unique and attractive banking system that combines stability, secrecy, and sophistication.

Asset Protection Strategies in Liechtenstein's Legal Framework

Liechtenstein, a tiny country nestled in the heart of Europe, has long been renowned for its secret banking system and its ability to provide a haven for the wealthy and privileged. This subchapter explores the various asset protection strategies available within Liechtenstein's legal framework, offering invaluable insights for diplomats and economists seeking to navigate its unique financial landscape.

One of the key attractions of Liechtenstein's banking system is its robust asset protection laws. The country's legal framework provides a range of options for safeguarding assets, including trusts, foundations, and corporations. These structures offer individuals and families a high level of confidentiality and protection, shielding their wealth from potential risks and creditors.

Trusts are particularly popular in Liechtenstein as they provide a flexible and secure means of asset protection. By transferring assets to a trust, individuals can ensure their wealth is managed and preserved for future generations. Trusts also offer enhanced privacy, as they are not subject to public disclosure requirements, making them an attractive option for those seeking to maintain a low profile.

Foundations, on the other hand, provide a unique combination of asset protection and philanthropy. Liechtenstein's legal framework allows for the establishment of private foundations, which can serve as a vehicle for managing and protecting assets while also enabling individuals to support charitable causes. This dual purpose makes foundations an appealing choice for individuals looking to align their wealth management strategies with their personal values.

Liechtenstein's banking system also offers a range of investment opportunities tailored to the needs of high-net-worth individuals. With its strong financial sector and stable economic environment, Liechtenstein provides a wealth of possibilities for investors looking to diversify their portfolios. Whether it's real estate, private equity, or alternative investments, Liechtenstein offers a range of options to suit different risk appetites and investment goals.

Furthermore, the regulatory framework and compliance standards in Liechtenstein's banking system ensure that investors can have confidence in the integrity of the financial sector. The country's commitment to transparency and adherence to international standards has earned it a reputation as a trusted and reputable offshore banking jurisdiction.

In conclusion, Liechtenstein's legal framework provides a range of asset protection strategies that cater to the unique needs of diplomats and economists. From trusts and foundations to investment opportunities and regulatory compliance, Liechtenstein's secret banking system offers unparalleled advantages for those seeking to safeguard their wealth and make the most of its financial sector. By understanding and leveraging these strategies, individuals can navigate the intricacies of Liechtenstein's banking system and secure their financial future.

Ensuring Long-term Stability through Asset Protection in Liechtenstein

Liechtenstein, a small fairy tale semi-constitutional monarchy nestled in the heart of Europe, boasts a secret banking system that has captivated the attention of diplomats and economists alike. Its offshore banking services, wealth management and private banking options, tax optimization strategies, asset protection and trust services, and investment opportunities in the financial sector have made it a preferred destination for wealthy individuals and families seeking a secure haven for their assets.

One of the key factors that sets Liechtenstein apart from other financial centers is its long-standing commitment to ensuring long-term stability through robust asset protection measures. With a strong regulatory framework and a culture of compliance, Liechtenstein's banking system has become synonymous with trustworthiness and security.

Asset protection and trust services play a pivotal role in safeguarding the wealth of individuals and families in Liechtenstein. By establishing trusts and foundations, individuals can shield their assets from potential risks and uncertainties. Liechtenstein's trust laws provide a high level of confidentiality and protection, making it an attractive jurisdiction for those seeking to preserve their wealth for future generations.

Furthermore, Liechtenstein's banking system offers a range of investment opportunities that cater to both conservative and adventurous investors. From traditional investment vehicles such as stocks and bonds to alternative investment options like real estate and private equity, Liechtenstein's financial sector provides a diverse range of choices to suit different risk appetites.

The role of Liechtenstein's royal family in maintaining the secrecy and stability of its banking system cannot be underestimated. Their long-standing commitment to preserving the privacy and integrity of the country's financial sector has earned the trust of individuals and institutions worldwide. This trust, coupled with Liechtenstein's reputation for strict compliance with international regulations, has cemented its position as a premier destination for international business transactions.

For wealthy individuals and families considering relocating to Liechtenstein, the country offers not only a secure banking system but also estate planning and inheritance solutions. With its well-established legal framework and favorable tax environment, Liechtenstein provides a conducive environment for individuals to plan their estates and ensure a smooth transfer of wealth to future generations.

In conclusion, Liechtenstein's secret banking system offers diplomats and economists a fascinating glimpse into a world of financial sophistication and stability. Its commitment to long-term asset protection, wealth management, and private banking services, combined with its regulatory framework and compliance culture, make it an ideal destination for those seeking a secure and confidential environment for their assets. Whether it's investment opportunities, estate planning, or international business transactions, Liechtenstein's banking system continues to be a beacon of stability and trust in an ever-changing global landscape.

Chapter 6: Investment Opportunities in Liechtenstein's Financial Sector

Overview of Liechtenstein's Financial Sector and its Growth Potential

Liechtenstein, a small yet prosperous nation nestled in the heart of Europe, has long been renowned for its secret banking system. This subchapter aims to provide diplomats and economists with a comprehensive overview of Liechtenstein's financial sector and shed light on its growth potential.

Liechtenstein's financial sector is an integral part of its economy, accounting for a significant portion of its GDP. The country's unique blend of political stability, favorable tax policies, and robust financial regulations has made it an attractive destination for individuals and businesses seeking financial services.

One of the key features of Liechtenstein's financial sector is its secret banking system, which has earned the country a reputation as a safe haven for wealth preservation and asset protection. The secrecy laws in Liechtenstein have historically been stringent, ensuring the privacy of clients and safeguarding their assets. However, recent global trends and international pressure have led Liechtenstein to adopt greater transparency measures and align its banking practices with international standards.

Despite these changes, Liechtenstein's financial sector continues to thrive. The country's banks offer a wide range of services, including private banking, wealth management, trust administration, and investment advisory. The sector is characterized by its expertise in catering to high-net-worth individuals, offering personalized solutions tailored to their unique financial needs.

Liechtenstein's financial sector has also shown remarkable resilience in the face of global economic challenges. The country's banks have weathered the storms of financial crises, thanks to their conservative approach to risk management and prudent investment strategies. This stability has further bolstered Liechtenstein's reputation as a reliable and trustworthy financial center.

Looking ahead, Liechtenstein's financial sector holds immense growth potential. The country has been actively diversifying its financial services, expanding into areas such as fintech, blockchain, and sustainable finance. Liechtenstein's forward-thinking approach, coupled with its supportive regulatory framework, positions it as a leader in these emerging sectors.

Moreover, Liechtenstein's strategic location within Europe provides it with a unique advantage. The country serves as a bridge between Switzerland and the European Union, making it an ideal hub for cross-border financial transactions. As global economic integration continues to deepen, Liechtenstein's financial sector is poised to benefit from increased international trade and investment flows.

In conclusion, Liechtenstein's financial sector is a crucial component of its economy, known for its secret banking system and robust regulations. It offers a wide range of services, catering to high-net-worth individuals and businesses. Despite recent transparency measures, Liechtenstein's financial sector remains strong and resilient. Looking ahead, the sector holds significant growth potential, driven by its diversification into emerging sectors and its strategic location within Europe. Diplomats and economists should closely monitor Liechtenstein's financial sector as it continues to evolve and shape the country's economic landscape.

Investment Options and Opportunities in Liechtenstein's Financial Markets

Liechtenstein's financial markets offer a plethora of investment options and opportunities for diplomats and economists looking to explore the country's secret banking system. Known for its fairy tale semi-constitutional monarchy, Liechtenstein has carved a niche for itself in the offshore banking industry, providing exceptional banking services, wealth management, and private banking solutions.

One of the key draws of Liechtenstein's financial sector is its tax optimization strategies. With a favorable tax regime, individuals and businesses can benefit from various tax planning tools and structures, allowing them to minimize their tax liabilities while maximizing their returns. This unique feature has attracted numerous wealthy individuals and families who seek to optimize their wealth and protect their assets.

When it comes to investment opportunities, Liechtenstein's financial markets present a diverse range of options. Investors can choose from a wide array of asset classes, including stocks, bonds, real estate, and alternative investments such as hedge funds and private equity. The country's regulatory framework ensures transparency and compliance, providing a secure environment for investment activities.

Furthermore, Liechtenstein's banking system facilitates international business transactions, making it an ideal hub for conducting cross-border trade and investments. The country's well-established infrastructure and efficient financial services enable seamless transactions and facilitate global business activities.

The role of Liechtenstein's royal family cannot be overlooked in maintaining the secrecy and stability of its banking system. Their commitment to upholding the reputation of Liechtenstein as a global financial center has significantly contributed to the country's success in attracting international clients and investors.

For diplomats and economists interested in wealth preservation and estate planning, Liechtenstein offers a range of asset protection and trust services. These services ensure the safeguarding of assets for future generations, providing peace of mind and long-term financial security.

As Liechtenstein continues to evolve and adapt to the changing global financial landscape, it remains an attractive destination for individuals and businesses seeking a secure and confidential banking system. The country's commitment to maintaining a robust regulatory framework and fostering a culture of innovation makes it a compelling choice for those looking to explore investment opportunities in a stable and secretive financial jurisdiction.

In conclusion, the investment options and opportunities in Liechtenstein's financial markets are vast and varied. From offshore banking services to wealth management and asset protection, the country's banking system caters to the unique needs of diplomats, economists, and wealthy individuals alike. With its favorable tax regime, efficient regulatory framework, and commitment to secrecy, Liechtenstein continues to be a prominent player in the global financial landscape.

Case Studies on Successful Investments in Liechtenstein

Liechtenstein, the fairy tale semi-constitutional monarchy known for its secret banking system, has long been a haven for wealthy individuals, families, and international businesses seeking offshore banking services. With its robust wealth management and private banking sector, as well as attractive tax optimization strategies, Liechtenstein offers a plethora of investment opportunities in its financial sector.

In this subchapter, we will delve into case studies that highlight successful investments made in Liechtenstein. These real-life examples will showcase the benefits and potential returns of investing in the country's banking system, shedding light on the reasons why diplomats and economists should consider Liechtenstein as a strategic investment destination.

One prominent case study revolves around a wealthy family from Europe who relocated to Liechtenstein to take advantage of its banking system. By establishing trusts and utilizing asset protection services, the family was able to safeguard their wealth while optimizing their tax liabilities. The stability and discretion offered by Liechtenstein's regulatory framework proved crucial in preserving their assets for future generations.

Another case study focuses on an international business that leveraged Liechtenstein's banking system to facilitate seamless cross-border transactions. By utilizing the expertise of local financial institutions, the business was able to navigate complex regulatory landscapes and streamline their international operations. This case study will provide insights into the value-added services offered by Liechtenstein's financial sector to support international business transactions.

Additionally, we will explore the role of Liechtenstein's royal family in maintaining the secrecy and stability of its banking system. This unique aspect sets Liechtenstein apart from other offshore banking jurisdictions and provides an added layer of trust and confidence for investors. By understanding the royal family's commitment to upholding the integrity of the banking system, diplomats and economists can gain a deeper appreciation for the sustainability of investments made in Liechtenstein.

Through these case studies, diplomats and economists will gain valuable insights into the investment opportunities, regulatory framework, compliance standards, and wealth management services available in Liechtenstein. Whether it be estate planning, wealth preservation, or international business transactions, Liechtenstein offers a range of solutions tailored to the needs of individuals and businesses alike.

By considering the success stories of others, diplomats and economists can make informed decisions and capitalize on the unique advantages offered by Liechtenstein's secret banking system. With its combination of financial stability, confidentiality, and expertise, Liechtenstein continues to attract investors seeking long-term growth and security for their wealth.

Risk Management and Mitigation Strategies in Liechtenstein's Financial Sector

Introduction:

Liechtenstein's financial sector has long been shrouded in mystery, with its secret banking system attracting both intrigue and admiration. However, with great secrecy comes great responsibility, and the need for robust risk management and mitigation strategies is crucial to maintain stability and trust in the sector. This subchapter aims to provide valuable insights into the risk management practices employed in Liechtenstein's financial sector and the mitigation strategies employed to safeguard the interests of its clients.

Risk Management in Liechtenstein's Financial Sector:

Liechtenstein's banking system operates within a well-defined regulatory framework that promotes transparency, stability, and compliance. Key risks that are addressed in this sector include credit risk, market risk, liquidity risk, operational risk, and reputation risk. Diplomats and economists will find it interesting to explore how these risks are identified, assessed, and managed effectively.

Mitigation Strategies:

Liechtenstein's financial sector has implemented various mitigation strategies to ensure the smooth functioning of its banking system. These strategies include diversification of investment portfolios, stress testing, robust internal control systems, and strict adherence to international standards and regulations. By adopting these measures, Liechtenstein's banks aim to mitigate risks and safeguard the interests of their clients.

Furthermore, measures like comprehensive due diligence, know-your-customer (KYC) procedures, and enhanced anti-money laundering (AML) practices are implemented to prevent illicit activities and maintain the integrity of the financial system. These strategies are of particular interest to diplomats and economists who seek to understand the mechanisms that ensure the legitimacy and security of offshore banking services in Liechtenstein.

Collaboration and International Cooperation:

Liechtenstein recognizes the importance of international collaboration in managing risks effectively. The country actively engages in international regulatory forums and cooperates with other jurisdictions to combat financial crimes, promote transparency, and exchange information. Diplomats and economists will benefit from understanding the collaborative efforts undertaken by Liechtenstein's financial sector to strengthen its risk management practices.

Conclusion:

Liechtenstein's financial sector has built a reputation for its secret banking system, attracting wealthy individuals, families, and international businesses. However, maintaining this reputation requires a robust risk management framework and effective mitigation strategies. By exploring the risk management practices and mitigation strategies employed in Liechtenstein's financial sector, diplomats and economists gain valuable insights into how this fairy tale semi-constitutional monarchy continues to ensure the stability, security, and prosperity of its banking system.

Chapter 7: Regulatory Framework and Compliance in Liechtenstein's Banking System

Overview of Liechtenstein's Regulatory Landscape for Banking

Liechtenstein, a small European country nestled between Switzerland and Austria, has long been known for its secretive and highly-regarded banking system. In this subchapter, we will explore the regulatory landscape that governs Liechtenstein's banking sector, providing diplomats and economists with a comprehensive understanding of the country's unique financial environment.

Liechtenstein's regulatory framework for banking is characterized by a combination of strict regulations and a commitment to maintaining client confidentiality. The Financial Market Authority (FMA) is the primary regulatory body responsible for overseeing the country's banking sector. The FMA ensures compliance with international standards and best practices, while also safeguarding the reputation and stability of Liechtenstein's financial system.

One of the key features of Liechtenstein's banking system is its emphasis on transparency and due diligence. Banks operating in the country are required to adhere to stringent anti-money laundering (AML) and know-your-customer (KYC) regulations. This ensures that only legitimate funds are accepted, and that the identities of clients are thoroughly verified. Additionally, the FMA conducts regular audits and inspections to ensure compliance with these regulations.

Liechtenstein's banking system also offers a wide range of services tailored to meet the needs of high-net-worth individuals and families. Wealth management and private banking services are a specialty of Liechtenstein, providing clients with personalized investment strategies and asset protection solutions. The country's favorable tax optimization strategies further attract individuals and businesses seeking to minimize their tax liabilities.

Moreover, Liechtenstein offers a robust framework for asset protection and trust services. Trusts and foundations are commonly utilized to safeguard assets, manage wealth, and facilitate estate planning and inheritance solutions. The country's legal system provides a solid foundation for these structures, ensuring the protection of assets and the smooth transfer of wealth between generations.

Investment opportunities in Liechtenstein's financial sector are also worth exploring. The country boasts a stable and prosperous economy, with a strong focus on innovation and technology. Various investment vehicles, such as venture capital funds and private equity firms, enable investors to tap into the country's thriving business landscape.

It is important to note that Liechtenstein's banking system operates within the framework of a semi-constitutional monarchy. The royal family, with their long-standing commitment to maintaining the secrecy and stability of the banking system, plays a crucial role in preserving the country's reputation and attracting wealthy individuals and businesses.

In conclusion, Liechtenstein's regulatory landscape for banking is characterized by a combination of strict regulations, transparency, and a commitment to client confidentiality. The country's banking system offers a wide array of services tailored to the needs of high-net-worth individuals and families, providing wealth management, tax optimization, asset protection, and investment opportunities. With its stable economy and the support of the royal family, Liechtenstein's banking system continues to attract diplomats and economists seeking to understand and engage with its unique financial environment.

Compliance Requirements and Regulatory Standards in Liechtenstein

Liechtenstein, a small fairy tale semi-constitutional monarchy nestled in the heart of Europe, is known for its secret banking system. This system has attracted diplomats and economists alike, who are intrigued by its unique offerings and opportunities. However, in order to navigate through this secretive yet highly regulated banking system, it is crucial to understand the compliance requirements and regulatory standards in Liechtenstein.

Offshore banking services in Liechtenstein are governed by a robust regulatory framework that ensures transparency and accountability. The Financial Market Authority (FMA) is the main regulatory body responsible for overseeing the banking sector in Liechtenstein. It sets strict compliance standards and conducts regular audits to ensure that banks adhere to these standards.

Wealth management and private banking in Liechtenstein are subject to stringent regulations aimed at protecting the interests of clients. Banks are required to follow the principles of due diligence, know-your-customer (KYC), and anti-money laundering (AML) measures. This ensures that the assets of clients are safeguarded and that the banking system is not exploited for illicit activities.

Tax optimization strategies in Liechtenstein are also subject to regulatory oversight. While Liechtenstein offers favorable tax incentives, it is important to comply with international tax standards and regulations. The country has been actively working towards implementing the OECD's Base Erosion and Profit Shifting (BEPS) framework to prevent tax avoidance and ensure fair taxation.

Asset protection and trust services in Liechtenstein are governed by the Liechtenstein Trust Law, which provides a strong legal framework for the establishment and administration of trusts. This ensures that assets are protected and can be passed on to future generations without any complications.

Investment opportunities in Liechtenstein's financial sector are subject to regulatory scrutiny to ensure investor protection. The Financial Market Authority monitors investment activities and enforces compliance with regulations such as the Markets in Financial Instruments Directive (MiFID II).

Liechtenstein's banking system plays a crucial role in facilitating international business transactions. Banks in Liechtenstein adhere to international compliance standards, such as the Foreign Account Tax Compliance Act (FATCA) and the Common Reporting Standard (CRS), to ensure the transparency of cross-border transactions.

The secrecy and stability of Liechtenstein's banking system are maintained not only by its regulatory framework but also by the active involvement of its royal family. The royal family has played a key role in establishing and maintaining the reputation of Liechtenstein as a reliable and discreet financial hub.

In conclusion, Liechtenstein's secret banking system offers lucrative opportunities for diplomats and economists, but it is essential to understand and comply with the compliance requirements and regulatory standards in place. The country's robust regulatory framework ensures transparency, accountability, and the protection of clients' interests, making Liechtenstein an attractive destination for wealth management, private banking, and international business transactions.

Anti-Money Laundering (AML) and Know Your Customer (KYC) Measures in Liechtenstein

Liechtenstein's secret banking system has long been a subject of intrigue and fascination for diplomats and economists alike. Known for its fairy tale semi-constitutional monarchy and its reputation as an offshore banking haven, Liechtenstein offers a unique blend of wealth management, private banking, and tax optimization strategies. However, behind this glamorous facade lies a robust regulatory framework that ensures compliance and safeguards against money laundering and illicit financial activities.

The Anti-Money Laundering (AML) and Know Your Customer (KYC) measures in Liechtenstein are of utmost importance to maintain the integrity and stability of its banking system. These measures are designed to prevent the misuse of the financial system for money laundering, terrorist financing, and other criminal activities. Liechtenstein's commitment to combating financial crimes is evident in its strict adherence to international standards and its continuous efforts to enhance its regulatory framework.

For diplomats and economists seeking to understand the intricacies of Liechtenstein's banking system, it is crucial to have a comprehensive understanding of the AML and KYC measures in place. This subchapter aims to shed light on the key aspects of these measures and their significance in Liechtenstein's financial sector.

In Liechtenstein, AML regulations are enforced by the Financial Market Authority (FMA) and the Financial Intelligence Unit (FIU), which work in close cooperation with international bodies such as the Financial Action Task Force (FATF). Financial institutions are required to implement robust AML policies and procedures, including customer due diligence, transaction monitoring, and reporting of suspicious activities. These measures ensure that the source of funds is legitimate and that transactions are conducted transparently.

The KYC process is an integral part of AML measures in Liechtenstein. It requires financial institutions to obtain and verify essential information about their customers, including their identity, source of wealth, and business activities. By conducting thorough due diligence on customers, Liechtenstein's banks can mitigate the risks associated with money laundering and maintain the integrity of the financial system.

Liechtenstein's commitment to AML and KYC measures goes hand in hand with its dedication to maintaining the secrecy and stability of its banking system. The role of the royal family in upholding these values cannot be understated. Their unwavering support and oversight contribute to the trust and confidence placed in Liechtenstein's financial sector.

In conclusion, the AML and KYC measures in Liechtenstein are crucial components of its banking system. Diplomats and economists interested in Liechtenstein's secret banking system must familiarize themselves with these measures to understand the regulatory framework and compliance requirements. By doing so, they can gain insights into the mechanisms that ensure the integrity and stability of Liechtenstein's financial sector, making it an attractive destination for wealthy individuals, families, and international business transactions.

Maintaining Transparency and Trust in Liechtenstein's Banking System

Liechtenstein's banking system has long been shrouded in secrecy, earning it the reputation of being a safe haven for wealthy individuals and families seeking to protect their assets. However, in recent years, there has been a growing demand for increased transparency and trust in the banking industry, both globally and within Liechtenstein itself. This subchapter aims to explore the measures taken by Liechtenstein to maintain transparency and trust in its banking system, catering specifically to diplomats and economists who are keen to understand the intricacies of this unique financial landscape.

Liechtenstein, known as a secret banking system in a fairy tale semi-constitutional monarchy, has recognized the need to adapt to changing global norms and regulations. In response to international pressure, Liechtenstein has implemented a robust regulatory framework and compliance system that ensures the highest standards of transparency and accountability. This includes strict anti-money laundering measures, customer due diligence procedures, and comprehensive reporting requirements.

Furthermore, Liechtenstein has actively promoted wealth management and private banking services, offering a wide range of financial products and solutions tailored to the needs of its diverse clientele. The country's offshore banking services have become a magnet for individuals and businesses looking to optimize their tax strategies while benefiting from the stability and expertise of Liechtenstein's financial sector.

In order to safeguard the interests of its clients, Liechtenstein has also prioritized asset protection and trust services. The country's legal framework provides a solid foundation for individuals and families seeking to protect their wealth through trusts and foundations. Coupled with the country's political stability and strong rule of law, Liechtenstein offers a secure environment for long-term wealth preservation.

Liechtenstein's banking system also plays a vital role in facilitating international business transactions. The country's well-established network of correspondent banks and its commitment to maintaining high standards of compliance make it an attractive destination for cross-border trade and investment. Diplomats and economists can explore the investment opportunities available within Liechtenstein's financial sector, which range from traditional asset classes to alternative investments such as fintech and sustainable finance.

Finally, it is worth mentioning the crucial role played by Liechtenstein's royal family in maintaining the secrecy and stability of its banking system. The royal family's commitment to the principality's financial sector and their active involvement in promoting transparency and trust further enhances Liechtenstein's reputation as a reliable and secure banking destination.

In conclusion, Liechtenstein's banking system has successfully adapted to changing global demands by prioritizing transparency and trust. Through its regulatory framework, wide range of financial services, and commitment to compliance, Liechtenstein continues to attract diplomats, economists, and wealthy individuals who seek a banking system that combines security, stability, and transparency.

Chapter 8: Wealthy Individuals and Families Relocating to Liechtenstein for its Banking System

The Appeal of Liechtenstein for High Net Worth Individuals and Families

Liechtenstein, a small principality nestled in the heart of Europe, has long captivated the attention of high net worth individuals and families seeking a discreet and secure banking system. Renowned for its fairy tale-like landscape and semi-constitutional monarchy, Liechtenstein boasts a secret banking system that has become the envy of the world.

For diplomats and economists who are intrigued by the enigma of Liechtenstein's secret banking system, this subchapter explores the various facets that make this principality a magnet for the wealthy.

One of the key draws for high net worth individuals and families is the offshore banking services offered in Liechtenstein. With a strong tradition of financial privacy and discretion, Liechtenstein's banks provide a safe haven for individuals looking to safeguard their assets from prying eyes. This level of secrecy is further enhanced by the country's strict regulatory framework and compliance standards, ensuring that the privacy of clients is always upheld.

In addition to offshore banking services, Liechtenstein is also renowned for its wealth management and private banking offerings. With a plethora of investment opportunities in the financial sector, individuals and families can benefit from tailored investment strategies that are designed to optimize tax planning and asset protection. Liechtenstein's expertise in trust services further enhances the appeal of its banking system, providing individuals with comprehensive solutions for estate planning and inheritance matters.

Another unique aspect of Liechtenstein's banking system is its role in facilitating international business transactions. With its strategic location in the heart of Europe, Liechtenstein offers a gateway for global trade and investment. The stability and reliability of its banking system, coupled with the expertise of its financial institutions, make Liechtenstein an attractive destination for businesses looking to expand their international reach.

Finally, the role of Liechtenstein's royal family cannot be understated in maintaining the secrecy and stability of its banking system. With a deep-rooted commitment to preserving the country's reputation as a financial safe haven, the royal family has played a pivotal role in shaping Liechtenstein's banking sector into what it is today.

In conclusion, Liechtenstein's secret banking system holds immense appeal for high net worth individuals and families, as well as diplomats and economists. With its offshore banking services, wealth management and private banking offerings, tax optimization strategies, and asset protection and trust services, Liechtenstein provides a comprehensive solution for those seeking financial privacy and security. Furthermore, the country's role in facilitating international business transactions, coupled with the unwavering commitment of its royal family, further enhances the allure of Liechtenstein's banking system.

Relocation Services and Benefits for Wealthy Individuals in Liechtenstein

Liechtenstein, a small yet prosperous country nestled amid the majestic Alps, has long been renowned for its secret banking system. In recent years, it has evolved into a preferred destination for wealthy individuals seeking offshore banking services, wealth management, and private banking. This subchapter explores the relocation services and benefits available to these discerning individuals who choose to make Liechtenstein their new home.

For diplomats and economists seeking a comprehensive understanding of Liechtenstein's banking system, it is crucial to delve into the various aspects that make it an attractive option for wealthy individuals. One of the key advantages lies in the tax optimization strategies offered in Liechtenstein. With its favorable tax environment, individuals can benefit from reduced taxes on their wealth and income, ensuring maximum financial growth and protection.

Furthermore, Liechtenstein's asset protection and trust services provide an added layer of security for wealthy individuals looking to safeguard their assets from potential risks. The country's robust regulatory framework and compliance standards ensure transparency and accountability in the banking sector, instilling confidence in its stability and reliability.

A notable benefit for those relocating to Liechtenstein is the ease of international business transactions facilitated through its banking system. With a range of investment opportunities available, from real estate to innovative startups, individuals can capitalize on Liechtenstein's thriving financial sector while enjoying the country's strong economic and political stability.

Estate planning and inheritance solutions are also crucial considerations for wealthy individuals. Liechtenstein offers a comprehensive range of services in these areas, allowing individuals to structure their assets and manage their estates efficiently. This ensures a smooth transition of wealth to the next generation, while taking advantage of the country's favorable legal framework.

The role of Liechtenstein's royal family cannot be overlooked when analyzing the secrecy and stability of its banking system. The royal family has played a pivotal role in maintaining the country's reputation as a secure and discreet offshore banking destination. Their commitment to upholding the highest standards of confidentiality has further solidified Liechtenstein's position as a trusted financial hub.

In conclusion, Liechtenstein's relocation services and benefits for wealthy individuals are unparalleled. The country's secret banking system, combined with its tax optimization strategies, asset protection services, and investment opportunities, make it an ideal destination for diplomats and economists seeking to understand and capitalize on this unique financial ecosystem. Whether it is wealth management, estate planning, or international business transactions, Liechtenstein offers a fairy tale-like solution in a semi-constitutional monarchy, making it an attractive choice for the discerning elite.

Case Studies on Successful Relocations to Liechtenstein

Liechtenstein, a picturesque fairy tale semi-constitutional monarchy, has long been renowned for its secret banking system. Over the years, it has attracted numerous wealthy individuals and families, seeking offshore banking services, wealth management, asset protection, and tax optimization strategies. In this subchapter, we will explore some fascinating case studies of successful relocations to Liechtenstein and delve into the reasons behind their choices.

One notable case study is that of the Smith family, who relocated to Liechtenstein to take advantage of the country's exceptional wealth management and private banking services. Mr. Smith, a successful entrepreneur, was impressed by the extensive range of investment opportunities available in Liechtenstein's financial sector. With the guidance of local experts, he was able to diversify his portfolio, ensuring long-term financial stability.

Another intriguing case study involves the Johnsons, a family seeking asset protection and trust services. Concerned about the unpredictability of global markets, they turned to Liechtenstein, known for its robust regulatory framework and compliance in the banking sector. By establishing a trust, the Johnsons were able to safeguard their assets and ensure their long-term preservation for future generations.

Liechtenstein's banking system has also facilitated international business transactions for numerous companies. One such example is the relocation of a multinational corporation headquarters to Liechtenstein. The company recognized the advantages of conducting business in a secure and discreet environment, allowing them to navigate complex international regulations seamlessly.

The role of Liechtenstein's royal family cannot be overlooked in maintaining the secrecy and stability of its banking system. Their commitment to upholding the country's reputation as a global financial center has been instrumental in attracting high-net-worth individuals and businesses.

Estate planning and inheritance solutions are another key aspect of Liechtenstein's banking system. The Thompson family, for instance, chose to relocate to Liechtenstein to benefit from its favorable estate planning laws. By establishing a foundation, they were able to protect their assets, ensuring a smooth transfer to the next generation.

These case studies highlight the diverse reasons why wealthy individuals and families choose to relocate to Liechtenstein. Whether seeking privacy, asset protection, or international business opportunities, Liechtenstein's secret banking system offers a unique combination of services and advantages. With its strong regulatory framework, stable economy, and commitment to maintaining the secrecy of its banking system, Liechtenstein continues to attract diplomats, economists, and discerning individuals from around the world.

Integrating into Liechtenstein's Society and Culture as a Wealthy Individual

Liechtenstein, with its secret banking system and fairy tale semi-constitutional monarchy, offers a unique opportunity for wealthy individuals to establish themselves in a country known for its financial prowess and stability. However, assimilating into Liechtenstein's society and culture requires a nuanced understanding of its traditions, values, and social dynamics.

One of the key aspects of integrating into Liechtenstein's society is appreciating its commitment to privacy and discretion. As a wealthy individual, you will need to understand the importance of maintaining confidentiality in your financial affairs. Liechtenstein's banking system has thrived on its ability to protect the privacy of its clients, and respecting this tradition is crucial for building trust and credibility within the community.

Additionally, building connections with local residents is essential for successful integration. Liechtenstein is a close-knit community, and it is important to establish relationships with influential individuals, such as diplomats and economists, who can provide guidance and support. Attending social events, joining clubs, and participating in community initiatives can help foster these relationships and provide a deeper understanding of the local culture.

Understanding the role of the royal family is also vital in integrating into Liechtenstein's society. The royal family plays a significant role in maintaining the secrecy and stability of the banking system. Familiarizing yourself with their customs and traditions can help you navigate the social landscape more effectively and demonstrate your commitment to the country's values.

Furthermore, embracing the local language and culture will greatly enhance your integration experience. While many people in Liechtenstein speak English, making an effort to learn German, the official language, will showcase your dedication to becoming part of the community. Participating in cultural activities, such as attending festivals and visiting historical landmarks, will also deepen your appreciation for Liechtenstein's rich heritage.

Finally, engaging with the local economy and contributing to the community will solidify your place in Liechtenstein society. Investing in local businesses and supporting philanthropic initiatives will not only demonstrate your commitment to the country's growth but also help you establish a positive reputation among the locals.

In conclusion, integrating into Liechtenstein's society and culture as a wealthy individual requires a multifaceted approach. By understanding the importance of privacy, building connections, appreciating the role of the royal family, embracing the local language and culture, and engaging with the local economy, you can successfully establish yourself in Liechtenstein and benefit from its thriving banking system while contributing to the overall development of the country.

Chapter 9: Estate Planning and Inheritance Solutions in Liechtenstein

Estate Planning Considerations for Foreign Investors in Liechtenstein

Liechtenstein, known for its secret banking system and fairy tale semi-constitutional monarchy, has become an attractive destination for foreign investors seeking offshore banking services, wealth management, and private banking. As diplomats and economists delve into the intricacies of Liechtenstein's financial sector, it is essential to understand the estate planning considerations that come with investing in this unique jurisdiction.

One of the key advantages of Liechtenstein's banking system is its comprehensive asset protection and trust services. When it comes to estate planning, establishing trusts can be a powerful tool for foreign investors. Liechtenstein's trust laws offer flexibility, confidentiality, and robust asset protection mechanisms, making it an ideal jurisdiction for creating trusts to safeguard wealth for future generations.

Furthermore, Liechtenstein offers various tax optimization strategies for foreign investors. Through careful estate planning, individuals can take advantage of tax benefits such as reduced inheritance tax rates, wealth tax exemptions, and favorable tax treatment for foundations and trusts. These strategies can help preserve and grow wealth while minimizing the tax burden on beneficiaries.

For wealthy individuals and families considering relocation to Liechtenstein, understanding the estate planning and inheritance solutions available is crucial. Liechtenstein's legal framework provides options such as dynastic trusts, which allow assets to be held in perpetuity, ensuring long-term wealth preservation and succession planning.

In addition to domestic considerations, Liechtenstein's banking system facilitates international business transactions. Foreign investors can leverage Liechtenstein's financial infrastructure to structure cross-border investments, manage global assets, and engage in international trade. Estate planning should take into account the international nature of investments, ensuring seamless transfer of assets across jurisdictions and minimizing potential tax and legal complications.

It is also important to note the role of Liechtenstein's royal family in maintaining the secrecy and stability of its banking system. The royal family's commitment to preserving the confidentiality and integrity of Liechtenstein's financial sector has been instrumental in attracting foreign investors. Diplomats and economists should appreciate the unique relationship between the monarchy and the banking system when advising clients on estate planning matters.

In conclusion, estate planning considerations for foreign investors in Liechtenstein necessitate a thorough understanding of the jurisdiction's asset protection and trust services, tax optimization strategies, international business transactions, and the role of the royal family. By harnessing the advantages offered by Liechtenstein's banking system, investors can ensure the preservation and seamless transfer of wealth for generations to come.

Trust and Foundation Structures for Efficient Inheritance Solutions

In the realm of wealth management and private banking, Liechtenstein has emerged as a fairy tale destination, offering a secret banking system that combines the charm of a semi-constitutional monarchy with offshore banking services. Diplomats and economists seeking to navigate this unique landscape will find valuable insights in this subchapter, which explores the role of trust and foundation structures in achieving efficient inheritance solutions.

Liechtenstein's banking system is renowned for its ability to provide comprehensive asset protection and trust services. With its strong regulatory framework and commitment to compliance, the country offers a secure environment for wealthy individuals and families looking to preserve and grow their wealth. Trust and foundation structures play a pivotal role in this process, allowing for effective estate planning and inheritance solutions.

One of the key advantages of using trusts in Liechtenstein is their flexibility. Trusts can be tailored to meet the specific needs and objectives of individuals and families, ensuring that their assets are managed and distributed according to their wishes. Trusts also offer a high degree of confidentiality, enabling individuals to protect their wealth from prying eyes.

Foundations, on the other hand, provide an additional layer of protection and stability. Liechtenstein's foundation law offers a unique blend of civil law and common law principles, making it an attractive option for those seeking a robust and reliable structure for wealth management. Foundations can be used to hold assets, manage investments, and facilitate international business transactions, all while maintaining the utmost privacy and confidentiality.

Moreover, Liechtenstein's royal family plays a crucial role in upholding the secrecy and stability of its banking system. Their longstanding commitment to maintaining the country's reputation as a safe haven for wealth has earned the trust and confidence of diplomats and economists alike.

For those considering relocation to Liechtenstein, the country's banking system provides a compelling reason to make the move. By leveraging the benefits of trust and foundation structures, individuals and families can optimize their tax strategies, protect their assets, and ensure a smooth and efficient transfer of wealth to future generations.

In conclusion, this subchapter sheds light on the trust and foundation structures that lie at the heart of Liechtenstein's secret banking system. Diplomats and economists will find valuable insights into the wealth management and inheritance solutions available in this fairy tale destination. By embracing the opportunities offered by trusts and foundations, individuals and families can navigate the complexities of international finance while safeguarding their wealth for generations to come.

Tax Optimization Strategies for Estate Planning in Liechtenstein

Estate planning is a crucial aspect of financial management, especially for individuals with significant assets and wealth. In Liechtenstein, a fairy tale semi-constitutional monarchy known for its secret banking system, there are several tax optimization strategies that can be employed to ensure the smooth transfer of wealth to future generations. This subchapter will explore the various techniques and solutions available to diplomats and economists who are interested in utilizing Liechtenstein's banking system for estate planning purposes.

One of the primary advantages of estate planning in Liechtenstein is the favorable tax regime. Liechtenstein offers a range of tax benefits, including low inheritance and gift taxes, making it an attractive jurisdiction for individuals looking to preserve their wealth. By structuring assets within Liechtenstein's banking system, diplomats and economists can effectively minimize their tax liabilities, ensuring that more of their wealth is passed on to their heirs.

Another tax optimization strategy available in Liechtenstein is the use of trusts. Liechtenstein has a long-standing tradition of trust services, and trusts can be an effective tool for estate planning. By transferring assets into a trust, individuals can retain control over their wealth while minimizing their tax obligations. Trusts in Liechtenstein also offer a high level of asset protection, ensuring that the wealth is safeguarded for future generations.

Additionally, Liechtenstein offers favorable tax treatment for foundations. Foundations can be established for various purposes, including philanthropy, family governance, and estate planning. By setting up a foundation, individuals can separate their assets from their personal estate, providing additional protection and flexibility in their wealth management strategies.

Furthermore, Liechtenstein's banking system provides a range of investment opportunities that can be utilized for estate planning purposes. Diplomats and economists can take advantage of Liechtenstein's financial sector to diversify their investment portfolios and maximize returns. The country's regulatory framework and compliance standards ensure transparency and stability, further enhancing the appeal of investing in Liechtenstein.

It is important to note that Liechtenstein's royal family plays a significant role in maintaining the secrecy and stability of its banking system. Their commitment to upholding the country's reputation as a safe and discreet financial center adds another layer of trust and confidence for individuals considering estate planning in Liechtenstein.

In conclusion, Liechtenstein's secret banking system offers diplomats and economists a range of tax optimization strategies for estate planning. By utilizing the country's favorable tax regime, trusts, foundations, and investment opportunities, individuals can effectively preserve and transfer their wealth to future generations. With the support of Liechtenstein's regulatory framework and the dedication of its royal family, estate planning in Liechtenstein provides a secure and reliable solution for individuals seeking to protect and grow their wealth.

Ensuring Smooth Succession and Inheritance in Liechtenstein

Liechtenstein is renowned for its secret banking system, drawing diplomats and economists alike to explore the intricacies of this fairy tale semi-constitutional monarchy. This chapter delves into a crucial aspect of Liechtenstein's financial landscape – ensuring smooth succession and inheritance.

In Liechtenstein, the importance of preserving wealth within families cannot be overstated. With its robust offshore banking services and wealth management options, individuals and families find themselves drawn to the principality as a hub for preserving and growing their assets. However, without careful estate planning and inheritance solutions, the fruits of their labor may be at risk.

Liechtenstein boasts an array of tax optimization strategies, asset protection, and trust services, all of which contribute to the seamless transfer of wealth across generations. By utilizing these services, wealthy individuals can safeguard their assets and minimize their tax liabilities, ensuring their heirs can enjoy the benefits of their hard-earned wealth.

The regulatory framework and compliance in Liechtenstein's banking system play a pivotal role in maintaining the stability and secrecy that so often attracts international business transactions. Diplomats and economists are well aware of the importance of a transparent and reliable financial sector, and Liechtenstein delivers on these fronts.

Another intriguing aspect lies in the role of Liechtenstein's royal family. Their commitment to maintaining the secrecy and stability of the banking system further solidifies the principality's allure. Their involvement ensures a sense of trust and continuity, making Liechtenstein an attractive destination for both domestic and international investors.

Moreover, Liechtenstein's financial sector offers a wide range of investment opportunities. The principality's strategic location, coupled with its favorable tax regulations, creates an environment ripe for investment. Diplomats and economists exploring the potential benefits of investing in Liechtenstein's financial sector can expect a favorable return on their investments.

For wealthy individuals and families contemplating relocation, Liechtenstein offers an enticing proposition. The combination of the secret banking system, favorable tax optimization strategies, and asset protection services make it an ideal destination for those seeking to manage and grow their wealth.

In conclusion, ensuring smooth succession and inheritance is a crucial component of Liechtenstein's banking system. With its comprehensive estate planning and inheritance solutions, Liechtenstein provides diplomats and economists with the peace of mind that their wealth will be preserved and transferred seamlessly. By embracing the principality's unique financial landscape, individuals and families can unlock the full potential of Liechtenstein's secret banking system.

Chapter 10: International Business Transactions Facilitated through Liechtenstein's Banking System

Liechtenstein's Role as a Gateway for International Business Transactions

Liechtenstein, a small principality nestled between Switzerland and Austria, has long been known for its secret banking system. This fairy tale semi-constitutional monarchy has successfully positioned itself as a global hub for offshore banking services, wealth management, private banking, and asset protection. In this subchapter, we will delve into the various aspects of Liechtenstein's role as a gateway for international business transactions, examining the lucrative opportunities it offers to diplomats and economists alike.

Liechtenstein's secret banking system has gained significant attention, attracting wealthy individuals and families from around the world who seek to optimize their taxes and protect their assets. The principality's favorable tax optimization strategies make it an attractive destination for those looking to enhance their financial standing. Moreover, the regulatory framework and compliance standards in Liechtenstein's banking system ensure transparency and stability, providing diplomats and economists with a secure environment to conduct business.

The wealth management and private banking services offered in Liechtenstein are renowned for their excellence. With a deep understanding of the unique needs and expectations of high-net-worth individuals, Liechtenstein's financial sector provides tailored solutions to preserve and grow wealth. The expertise of professionals in this sector, coupled with the principality's commitment to confidentiality, makes Liechtenstein an ideal choice for diplomats and economists seeking top-notch banking services.

For international business transactions, Liechtenstein serves as a strategic gateway. Its banking system facilitates seamless cross-border transactions, allowing businesses to expand their global reach. The reliability and efficiency of Liechtenstein's financial infrastructure enable diplomats and economists to navigate complex international trade and investment transactions effortlessly. The principality's role as a global financial intermediary cannot be underestimated.

Behind the success of Liechtenstein's secret banking system lies the role of its royal family. The monarchy has played a vital role in maintaining the secrecy and stability of the banking system, enhancing trust and confidence among clients. The royal family's commitment to upholding the principality's reputation as a safe haven for international financial transactions is a testament to Liechtenstein's enduring success.

In conclusion, Liechtenstein's role as a gateway for international business transactions cannot be overstated. Its secret banking system, combined with its offshore banking services, wealth management solutions, tax optimization strategies, and asset protection offerings, make it an attractive destination for diplomats and economists. The principality's commitment to regulatory compliance, transparency, and stability further reinforces its appeal. Whether it is estate planning, investment opportunities, or international business transactions, Liechtenstein's banking system has proven itself to be a reliable partner for diplomats and economists seeking to enhance their financial standing in a secure and confidential environment.

Cross-Border Payments and Trade Financing in Liechtenstein

Liechtenstein, a small country nestled in the heart of Europe, is renowned for its secretive banking system and fairy tale-like semi-constitutional monarchy. This unique combination has made it a preferred destination for diplomats and economists seeking offshore banking services, wealth management, and private banking solutions.

One of the key aspects of Liechtenstein's banking system is its ability to facilitate cross-border payments and trade financing. With its strong regulatory framework and compliance measures, the country has become a hub for international business transactions.

Liechtenstein offers a range of services to support cross-border payments, including wire transfers, electronic funds transfers, and digital payment solutions. These services are not only efficient but also secure, thanks to the country's robust financial infrastructure and adherence to international financial regulations.

Furthermore, Liechtenstein's banking system provides trade financing options to businesses looking to expand their operations globally. Whether it's import/export financing, letters of credit, or documentary collections, Liechtenstein's financial institutions offer a wide array of trade finance solutions to meet the diverse needs of businesses.

The role of Liechtenstein's royal family in maintaining the secrecy and stability of its banking system cannot be undermined. The royal family has played a significant role in shaping and safeguarding the country's financial sector. Their commitment to maintaining the highest standards of confidentiality and discretion has attracted wealthy individuals and families who seek asset protection and trust services.

Moreover, Liechtenstein's banking system offers attractive tax optimization strategies for individuals and businesses. The country's favorable tax regime, coupled with its comprehensive network of double taxation agreements, makes it an ideal jurisdiction for those looking to minimize their tax liabilities while ensuring compliance with international tax laws.

For diplomats and economists interested in investment opportunities, Liechtenstein's financial sector provides a range of options. From real estate and infrastructure projects to venture capital and private equity investments, the country offers a conducive environment for both domestic and foreign investors.

In addition, Liechtenstein's banking system caters to the unique needs of wealthy individuals and families relocating to the country. With its expertise in estate planning and inheritance solutions, Liechtenstein ensures the preservation and smooth transfer of wealth across generations.

To sum up, Liechtenstein's banking system is a well-established and highly sought-after destination for cross-border payments and trade financing. Its commitment to secrecy, stability, and compliance, coupled with its attractive tax optimization strategies and investment opportunities, make it a preferred choice for diplomats, economists, and those seeking a secure and efficient financial hub.

Mitigating Risks and Ensuring Compliance in International Business Transactions

In the fast-paced world of international business transactions, mitigating risks and ensuring compliance is of paramount importance. This subchapter delves into the strategies and measures that diplomats and economists need to be aware of when navigating Liechtenstein's secret banking system. With its fairy tale semi-constitutional monarchy and reputation as an offshore banking haven, Liechtenstein offers a unique landscape for wealth management, private banking, tax optimization, asset protection, trust services, and investment opportunities. However, it is crucial to understand the regulatory framework and compliance requirements to safeguard the interests of wealthy individuals and families, as well as facilitate international business transactions.

Liechtenstein's banking system operates within a strong regulatory framework that promotes transparency and accountability. Diplomats and economists must familiarize themselves with the rules and regulations governing offshore banking services in Liechtenstein to ensure that compliance is maintained throughout the transaction process. This includes adhering to anti-money laundering (AML) and know-your-customer (KYC) regulations, as well as complying with international tax laws and reporting obligations.

Moreover, diplomats and economists should be aware of the role of Liechtenstein's royal family in maintaining the secrecy and stability of its banking system. The royal family's commitment to upholding the integrity of the financial sector ensures that Liechtenstein remains a trusted and secure destination for international business transactions.

Furthermore, this subchapter explores the intricacies of estate planning and inheritance solutions in Liechtenstein. With its favorable tax environment and robust legal framework, Liechtenstein offers a range of options for wealthy individuals and families seeking to protect and transfer their assets. Diplomats and economists must understand the nuances of these solutions to guide their clients effectively.

Lastly, international business transactions facilitated through Liechtenstein's banking system require a comprehensive understanding of the risks involved. Diplomats and economists must assess and mitigate these risks to safeguard their clients' interests. This includes conducting thorough due diligence on counterparties, understanding the legal and regulatory landscape of the jurisdictions involved, and implementing robust risk management strategies.

In conclusion, mitigating risks and ensuring compliance are essential components of international business transactions in Liechtenstein's secret banking system. Diplomats and economists must navigate the regulatory framework, understand the role of the royal family, and stay abreast of estate planning solutions. By doing so, they can provide valuable guidance to their clients while maintaining the secrecy and stability that Liechtenstein's banking system is known for.

Leveraging Liechtenstein's Banking System for Global Business Expansion

Liechtenstein, a small yet captivating country nestled between Austria and Switzerland, has long been known for its secretive and reliable banking system. This subchapter aims to shed light on how diplomats and economists can leverage Liechtenstein's banking system to expand global business operations successfully.

Liechtenstein: A Secret Banking System in a Fairy Tale Semi-constitutional Monarchy

Liechtenstein's banking system operates within the unique framework of a semi-constitutional monarchy, where the royal family plays a significant role in maintaining the secrecy and stability of the system. This combination of tradition and innovation has created an environment conducive to global business expansion.

Offshore Banking Services in Liechtenstein

Liechtenstein's offshore banking services are renowned for their confidentiality and security. Diplomats and economists can utilize these services to protect assets, optimize taxes, and facilitate international business transactions. The country's strict regulatory framework ensures compliance while offering flexibility to meet the diverse needs of clients.

Wealth Management and Private Banking in Liechtenstein

Liechtenstein's private banking sector is known for its personalized approach and expertise in wealth management. Diplomats and economists can benefit from the country's extensive range of investment opportunities, tailored financial solutions, and comprehensive asset protection strategies. The stability and reliability of Liechtenstein's banking system make it an attractive choice for high-net-worth individuals and families.

Tax Optimization Strategies in Liechtenstein

Liechtenstein offers various tax optimization strategies that can help diplomats and economists minimize their tax burdens while remaining fully compliant with international regulations. The country's favorable tax environment, coupled with its robust legal framework, ensures a transparent and efficient approach to tax planning.

Asset Protection and Trust Services in Liechtenstein

Liechtenstein's asset protection and trust services provide a secure and confidential platform for safeguarding assets and managing succession planning. Diplomats and economists can take advantage of these services to protect their wealth, ensure seamless inheritance solutions, and maintain family legacies for future generations.

Investment Opportunities in Liechtenstein's Financial Sector

Liechtenstein's financial sector offers a wide range of investment opportunities across various asset classes, including alternative investments, real estate, and sustainable finance. Diplomats and economists can explore these opportunities to diversify their portfolios and achieve long-term growth.

Regulatory Framework and Compliance in Liechtenstein's Banking System

Liechtenstein's banking system operates under a robust regulatory framework that ensures transparency, stability, and compliance with international standards. Diplomats and economists can navigate this system confidently, knowing that their financial activities are closely monitored and regulated.

Wealthy Individuals and Families Relocating to Liechtenstein for its Banking System

Liechtenstein's banking system has attracted wealthy individuals and families seeking a safe haven for their assets. The country's reputation for financial stability, confidentiality, and exceptional client service makes it an ideal destination for those looking to relocate and benefit from its banking system.

Estate Planning and Inheritance Solutions in Liechtenstein

Liechtenstein provides comprehensive estate planning and inheritance solutions that enable diplomats and economists to preserve and transfer their wealth efficiently. The country's trust structures and legal frameworks offer flexibility and protection, ensuring that assets are distributed according to their owners' wishes.

International Business Transactions Facilitated Through Liechtenstein's Banking System

Liechtenstein's banking system serves as a gateway for international business transactions, offering a wide range of financial services tailored to the needs of global enterprises. Diplomats and economists can leverage the country's expertise in cross-border transactions, trade finance, and foreign exchange services to facilitate seamless international business expansion.

The Role of Liechtenstein's Royal Family in Maintaining the Secrecy and Stability of its Banking System

Liechtenstein's royal family plays a crucial role in maintaining the secrecy and stability of the country's banking system. Their commitment to upholding the highest standards of confidentiality and their active involvement in shaping financial regulations ensure the continued trust and integrity of Liechtenstein's banking sector.

In conclusion, Liechtenstein's banking system offers diplomats and economists a unique opportunity to leverage its services for global business expansion. From offshore banking to wealth management, tax optimization, and asset protection, Liechtenstein's banking system provides a fairy tale-like environment for secure and successful international financial activities.

Chapter 11: The Role of Liechtenstein's Royal Family in Maintaining the Secrecy and Stability of its Banking System

The Historical Connection between Liechtenstein's Royal Family and Banking Secrecy

Liechtenstein, a small principality nestled between Switzerland and Austria, is often referred to as a fairy tale semi-constitutional monarchy. Known for its picturesque landscapes and rich history, Liechtenstein holds a unique place in the world of international finance due to its secret banking system. At the heart of this system lies a historical connection between Liechtenstein's royal family and banking secrecy.

The story dates back to the early 20th century when Liechtenstein's Prince Franz I recognized the potential of the country's banking sector. With a vision to transform Liechtenstein into a financial hub, he established the Liechtensteinische Landesbank in 1861. This marked the beginning of Liechtenstein's journey towards becoming a global player in offshore banking.

The royal family's involvement in the banking sector did not stop at the establishment of the Landesbank. Over the years, they actively supported and nurtured the growth of the banking industry, recognizing its significance in the country's economy. Their influence and connections played a crucial role in attracting wealthy individuals and families to entrust their assets to Liechtenstein's banks.

One of the key factors that contribute to the success of Liechtenstein's banking system is its strict adherence to banking secrecy. This tradition can be traced back to the royal family's commitment to protecting the privacy and interests of their clients. As the custodians of the nation's wealth, the royal family understood the importance of maintaining confidentiality in financial matters.

Liechtenstein's royal family, with their deep-rooted commitment to maintaining the secrecy and stability of the banking system, has been instrumental in shaping the regulatory framework and compliance measures that govern the industry. Their involvement ensures that the highest standards of professionalism and integrity are upheld, making Liechtenstein an attractive destination for wealthy individuals and families seeking to protect and grow their assets.

In recent years, Liechtenstein's banking system has evolved to cater to the changing needs of its clients. Wealth management, private banking, tax optimization strategies, asset protection, and trust services are just a few of the specialized services offered by Liechtenstein's banks. These services, coupled with the country's favorable regulatory environment, have made Liechtenstein a preferred destination for international business transactions and wealth preservation.

The historical connection between Liechtenstein's royal family and banking secrecy has played a pivotal role in establishing the country's reputation as a premier offshore banking destination. Today, diplomats and economists recognize Liechtenstein as a jurisdiction that offers a comprehensive range of financial services while upholding the highest standards of confidentiality and stability. As Liechtenstein continues to evolve and adapt to the changing global financial landscape, its royal family remains an integral part of the country's commitment to maintaining its position as a leader in the world of secret banking systems.

The Royal Family's Influence on the Stability and Development of Liechtenstein's Banking System

Liechtenstein has long been known for its secretive and stable banking system, which has attracted wealthy individuals, families, and international businesses seeking offshore banking services, wealth management, and asset protection. This chapter delves into the unique role of Liechtenstein's royal family in maintaining the secrecy and stability of its banking system, and how their influence has shaped its development over the years.

The Principality of Liechtenstein is a small, landlocked country nestled between Switzerland and Austria. It is governed by a semi-constitutional monarchy, with the Prince of Liechtenstein as the head of state. The royal family, led by Prince Hans-Adam II and his son Prince Alois, has played a pivotal role in the development of Liechtenstein's banking system, ensuring its stability and success in the global financial arena.

One of the key contributions of the royal family has been their unwavering commitment to maintaining the secrecy and confidentiality of the banking system. Liechtenstein's banking laws are designed to protect the privacy of its clients, making it an attractive destination for wealthy individuals and families seeking to safeguard their assets. The royal family has actively supported and defended these laws, ensuring that they remain intact despite increasing international pressure for transparency.

Moreover, the royal family has played a crucial role in shaping Liechtenstein's regulatory framework and compliance standards. In collaboration with the government, they have implemented robust regulations to prevent money laundering, tax evasion, and other illicit activities within the banking sector. This has resulted in Liechtenstein being recognized as a reputable and compliant jurisdiction, further enhancing its appeal to both clients and international businesses.

The royal family's influence extends beyond regulatory matters, as they have also actively promoted Liechtenstein's financial sector and attracted investment opportunities. Their international connections and diplomatic networks have facilitated partnerships with global financial institutions, encouraging foreign investment and fostering economic growth. This has allowed Liechtenstein to position itself as a prominent player in the global financial landscape.

Furthermore, the royal family's involvement in estate planning and inheritance solutions has provided added value to Liechtenstein's banking system. Through their expertise and knowledge, they have created a favorable environment for wealthy individuals and families to plan their estates and ensure smooth succession. This has cemented Liechtenstein's reputation as a trusted and reliable destination for wealth management and asset protection.

In conclusion, Liechtenstein's royal family has played a significant role in maintaining the secrecy and stability of its banking system. Their unwavering commitment to privacy, advocacy for robust regulations, promotion of the financial sector, and expertise in estate planning have all contributed to the success and attractiveness of Liechtenstein's banking system. Diplomats and economists can appreciate the unique influence and contributions of the royal family, making Liechtenstein a compelling case study in the world of offshore banking and wealth management.

Collaborative Efforts between the Royal Family and Financial Institutions in Liechtenstein

Liechtenstein, a small yet prosperous country nestled in the heart of Europe, has long been known for its secret banking system. This fairy tale semi-constitutional monarchy has managed to create a haven for offshore banking services, wealth management, private banking, tax optimization strategies, asset protection, trust services, and investment opportunities. However, the success of Liechtenstein's financial sector is not solely attributed to its robust regulatory framework and compliance measures. It is the collaborative efforts between the royal family and financial institutions that have played a crucial role in maintaining the secrecy and stability of the banking system.

The royal family of Liechtenstein, led by Prince Hans-Adam II, has been actively involved in shaping the country's financial sector. With a deep understanding of the importance of discretion and privacy in the world of banking, the royal family has worked closely with financial institutions to create an environment conducive to the needs of wealthy individuals and families.

One of the key areas where collaboration between the royal family and financial institutions has been evident is in estate planning and inheritance solutions. Liechtenstein's banking system offers a range of services that cater to the needs of high-net-worth individuals looking to protect and transfer their wealth. The royal family has played a pivotal role in ensuring that the legal and regulatory framework supports these services, providing a secure and reliable platform for estate planning.

Furthermore, the royal family has been instrumental in facilitating international business transactions through Liechtenstein's banking system. Their diplomatic ties and extensive network have allowed financial institutions to establish strong connections with foreign markets, attracting international clients and investors. This has not only boosted the country's economy but has also solidified Liechtenstein's position as a global financial hub.

In addition to their role in estate planning and international business transactions, the royal family has actively promoted the importance of wealth management and private banking. By endorsing these services, they have encouraged wealthy individuals and families to relocate to Liechtenstein, further bolstering the country's reputation as a premier destination for financial services.

The collaborative efforts between the royal family and financial institutions have undoubtedly contributed to the success of Liechtenstein's secret banking system. By working hand in hand, they have upheld the principles of discretion, stability, and security that are synonymous with Liechtenstein's financial sector. As diplomats and economists, it is essential to recognize and appreciate the pivotal role played by the royal family in maintaining the integrity and appeal of Liechtenstein's banking system.

Preserving the Legacy - Future Prospects for Liechtenstein's Banking System under the Royal Family's Guidance.

Liechtenstein: A Secret Banking System in a Fairy Tale Semi-constitutional Monarchy

Liechtenstein, a small yet prosperous nation nestled in the heart of Europe, has long been renowned for its secret banking system. With a semi-constitutional monarchy as its governing structure, Liechtenstein offers a unique blend of stability, discretion, and financial opportunity. At the heart of this system lies the royal family, whose guidance has played a pivotal role in preserving the legacy of Liechtenstein's banking sector.

Offshore banking services in Liechtenstein

Liechtenstein's offshore banking services have been a cornerstone of its financial sector. Its strict adherence to confidentiality and robust asset protection measures have made it a preferred destination for individuals and corporations seeking to safeguard their wealth. Under the watchful eye of the royal family, Liechtenstein's offshore banking services have continued to attract clients from around the world.

Wealth management and private banking in Liechtenstein

Liechtenstein's banking system boasts a strong focus on wealth management and private banking. With a wealth of expertise and a commitment to personalized service, Liechtenstein's banks cater to the unique needs of affluent individuals and families. The royal family's dedication to maintaining the highest standards of integrity and professionalism has further solidified Liechtenstein's reputation as a premier destination for wealth management and private banking.

Tax optimization strategies in Liechtenstein

One of the key advantages of Liechtenstein's banking system is its tax optimization strategies. Through the use of legal and transparent structures, individuals and businesses can minimize their tax liabilities while remaining compliant with international regulations. The royal family's support for a robust regulatory framework ensures that Liechtenstein's tax optimization strategies are sustainable and in line with global standards.

Asset protection and trust services in Liechtenstein

Liechtenstein's banking system offers a comprehensive range of asset protection and trust services. From establishing trusts to safeguarding assets from unforeseen circumstances, Liechtenstein's banks provide tailored solutions to meet the specific needs of their clients. With the royal family's commitment to stability and security, individuals and families can have confidence in the long-term preservation of their assets.

Investment opportunities in Liechtenstein's financial sector

Liechtenstein's financial sector offers a diverse range of investment opportunities. From venture capital to real estate, Liechtenstein provides a favorable environment for both domestic and international investors. The royal family's commitment to fostering economic growth and stability ensures that investment opportunities in Liechtenstein's financial sector remain attractive and lucrative.

Regulatory framework and compliance in Liechtenstein's banking system

Liechtenstein's banking system operates within a robust regulatory framework, which is continuously updated to meet evolving global standards. The royal family's commitment to compliance and transparency has earned Liechtenstein a reputation as a responsible and trustworthy financial center.

Wealthy individuals and families relocating to Liechtenstein for its banking system

Liechtenstein's banking system has become a magnet for wealthy individuals and families seeking to relocate. The allure of a stable political climate, a strong rule of law, and a discreet banking system has prompted many to make Liechtenstein their new home. The royal family's role in maintaining the secrecy and stability of the banking system is a key factor in attracting these high-net-worth individuals.

Estate planning and inheritance solutions in Liechtenstein

Liechtenstein's banking system offers comprehensive estate planning and inheritance solutions. With a range of trust and foundation structures, individuals can ensure the orderly transfer of assets to future generations. The royal family's commitment to preserving the legacy of Liechtenstein's banking system ensures that estate planning and inheritance solutions remain secure and reliable.

International business transactions facilitated through Liechtenstein's banking system

Liechtenstein's banking system plays a vital role in facilitating international business transactions. Its efficient and reliable infrastructure, coupled with the royal family's commitment to stability, ensures that businesses can conduct cross-border transactions with ease and confidence. The banking system's reputation for discretion and professionalism further enhances Liechtenstein's appeal as a hub for international business.

The role of Liechtenstein's royal family in maintaining the secrecy and stability of its banking system

The royal family of Liechtenstein has been instrumental in maintaining the secrecy and stability of the nation's banking system. Their unwavering commitment to the principles of discretion, security, and integrity has helped to nurture and protect Liechtenstein's reputation as a global financial center. Through their guidance, the royal family ensures that the legacy of Liechtenstein's banking system will endure for generations to come.

In conclusion, Liechtenstein's banking system, under the guidance of the royal family, has established itself as a world-class destination for financial services. With its secret banking system, wealth management expertise, tax optimization strategies, and asset protection services, Liechtenstein offers a unique blend of opportunities for individuals, families, and businesses alike. The royal family's commitment to preserving the legacy of Liechtenstein's banking system ensures that its future prospects remain bright, cementing its position as a leader in the global financial landscape.